D0049477

Less than a Minute to Go

LESS THAN A
MINUTE TO GO

THE SECRET TO WORLD-CLASS
PERFORMANCE IN SPORT,
BUSINESS AND EVERYDAY LIFE

Dr. Bill Thierfelder

SAINT BENEDICT+PRESS

Charlotte, North Carolina

Cataloging-in-Publication data on file with the Library of Congress.

ISBN: 978-1-61890-403-4

Published in the United States by
Saint Benedict Press, LLC
PO Box 410487
Charlotte, NC 28241
www.saintbenedictpress.com

Printed and bound in the United States of America.

For Mary, my one, my wife,
and for all of my good children,
Mary, Joseph, Elizabeth, John,
James, Thomas, Luke, Ann,
Peter and Matthew, who help
me to see the perfection of the
present moment.

And for the monks of
Belmont Abbey, who since
1876 have dedicated their
lives to the students of
Belmont Abbey College.

CONTENTS

Foreword by Coach Mike Krzyzewski ix

Introduction xi
The big picture.

PART ONE: PREPARING YOUR MIND TO WIN
*The most common mental obstacles that get in the way of
world-class performance.*

Chapter 1: All Work and No Play 3
Play is where world-class performance is born.

Chapter 2: Running on Empty. 17
Playing for all the wrong reasons.

Chapter 3: Unsportsmanlike Conduct 37
Belief determines emotion.

Chapter 4: Don't Just Stand There 57
Awareness and adaptation; the process of change.

Chapter 5: The Pressure's On 79
The power of words.

PART TWO: MAKING PEAK PERFORMANCE A COMMON OCCURRENCE

Only those that understand peak performance can repeat it often and on demand.

Chapter 6: Walking on Water 105
Peak performance happens when it is least expected.

Chapter 7: Instant Replay 127
Reproducing peak performance when it counts.

PART THREE: PLAYING WITH A PASSION THAT NEVER ENDS

The stronger your purpose the better your performance.

Chapter 8: O Captain! My Captain! 155
Virtuous performances.

Chapter 9: Playing Hurt 171
Pain without a purpose is intolerable to human beings.

Chapter 10: Less Than a Minute to Go 191
The deeper meaning.

FOREWORD

IT WAS more than a love for the game of basketball that inspired me to devote my life and career to coaching, it was a passion for teaching and learning. I believe that to be a great teacher, you have to be an ever-willing learner; the process is reciprocal. And the main topic I have enjoyed learning and teaching the most throughout my career is leadership.

I have been fortunate to meet some great leaders from many walks of life and I love to engage in discussions with them on the topic—to hear them explain their philosophies, to learn new techniques and see things from new perspectives and sometimes to find common leadership ground even when our backgrounds and fields are vastly different. I am committed to never ceasing to learn and it is this commitment, in part, that drives me to keep doing what I do.

Dr. Bill Thierfelder is one of the leaders whose lessons and thoughts on the subject I value and appreciate. He has an unparalleled understanding of what it takes for an individual to turn his or her peak performance into their standard. As a leader and as a mentor to athletes, he knows exactly how to be the kind of leader who can help people develop that standard.

I love the way that Bill talks about pressure. For some, it is a frightening word—a word that is accompanied by the fear of failure. In this book, Bill explains how to redefine pressure as an opportunity. Whether in sport, in business or in life, approaching pressure with excitement and confidence, as opposed to anxiety, is a critical step in becoming a top performer.

I also appreciate the way that Bill talks about expectations. I don't impose many "rules" with my teams. Instead, together we step toward becoming unique to that particular group at that particular time. The standards we develop are important—they define who we are and who we hope to become during the course of a season. But more important than the words and values we choose as ours is the fact that they are *ours*. The most important standard that an individual or team sets is the one that comes from the inside, not those that are imposed from the outside. We ought to be the ones to define who we are and, more than that, who we can and will become.

Bill's book is ultimately about setting one's own standards and making certain that the standards you set are worthy, that they challenge you to achieve a level where peak performance is not something sought and rarely found but, rather, where your best self is your most common self.

In this book, my friend Bill Thierfelder, a great leader and motivator, puts the words and descriptions to what we leaders try to do every day—to challenge ourselves and our teams to be at our best, all the time.

— Mike Krzyzewski, 2013

INTRODUCTION

THE sold-out crowd at Miami's Orange Bowl had started to celebrate. With six seconds remaining in the game and with Boston College down 45–41, the game was over. The reigning NCAA Division I National Champions, the University of Miami Hurricanes, had weathered an incredible shoot-out with the Boston College Eagles. All that remained was for BC to run their last play from the Miami forty-seven yard-line and the oranges would start flying. The only problem was that no one had told BC quarterback, Doug Flutie.

With twenty-eight seconds remaining in the game Flutie began the drive from his own twenty yard-line. His first thought was, "Given the time, I probably have four pass plays." World-class performers focus on what they can and will do. As he entered the huddle his confidence and resolve filled the team around him. Within two plays they were on the Miami forty-seven yard-line. The third pass fell incomplete, but to Flutie it was as if it had never happened. World-class performers remain focused in the present moment. Only six seconds remained in a game where both teams had combined for more than twelve-hundred yards of total offense. As Flutie came to the line, his eyes revealed a mind in control. He loved the game; he loved playing. And it showed. He was in the backyard with his buddies about to run everyone's favorite play: the last second Hail Mary.

The ball was snapped and Flutie dropped back to pass. Before he could get set, he saw All-American defensive linemen Jerome Brown lunging toward him. Flutie had an uncanny knack for slipping out of a defensive player's grasp at the last millisecond. Suddenly he was rolling out to his right, back to the BC thirty-five, with the defense closing in on him fast. In the melee Flutie never lost composure or focus. With determination and purpose he stepped toward the thirty-seven yard-line and threw a Hail Mary pass into a 30 mph headwind. The Miami defenders anticipated it, but that was the problem. They thought about what should happen rather than seeing what was happening. As they stood on the five yard line waiting to break-up the fifty yard pass that would never come they failed to recognize that the diminutive 5'10" 173 lb. quarterback had actually thrown a sixty-three yard pass. By the time they realized it the ball had sailed over their heads and straining finger tips into the waiting arms of Gerard Phelan who caught the miraculous pass with no time left on the clock. Touchdown!

The backyard joy of old erupted. The BC players exploded into celebration, jumping, hugging, yelling, whooping, and frolicking around the field of play. No amount of money, power, or fame could add to that moment. The sheer joy of playing their best was all that counted. Those other things may come later but they would be, at best, faint reminders of that mystical moment of play: where play and wisdom find common ground in the contemplation of the highest things; where they exist for their own sake and not for some mean and artificial end.

This is where the very best of world-class performance can cross over into a special realm known as peak performance: playing for its own sake with every skill, talent, and ability brought to bear in the present moment. The Greeks had a word for it, *arête*, meaning excellence or virtue. Aristotle said, "Excellence is an art won by training and habituation. We do not act rightly because we have virtue or excellence, but we rather have those because we have acted rightly. We are what we repeatedly do. Excellence, then, is not an act but a habit."

*   *   *   *   *

I once spoke to several hundred retired players at the Annual NFL Players Association Meeting, and I asked them, "How many of you during your careers were trying to perfect the intellectual virtue of art?" They looked at me as if to say, "Are you sure you're in the right place?" I smiled in an assuring way and asked them, "How many of you were trying to perfect yourselves as football players?" Everyone in the room raised their hands. "That," I said, "is the intellectual virtue of art." It is the right method of external production. It means that if you are trying to perfect yourself through your work in business, carpentry, football, or anything else, then you are engaged in the intellectual virtue of art.

However, art is only one of the virtues and virtues do not exist in isolation. You need prudence, for example, in order to have fortitude otherwise you will tend toward one of two extremes: cowardice or recklessness. The virtues are interconnected. The more of them you have the happier you will be and the better you will perform. The virtues also go hand-in-hand with being a great athlete, coach, worker, friend, spouse, or parent. Being any one of these is all about achieving excellence: virtue. You don't have to choose between being a world-class athlete and a saint. You can be—and hopefully desire to be—both. In fact, if you're striving to be a top athlete and a good person, you're already cultivating many virtues, like discipline, fortitude, prudence, and courage, among others.

But while sport can be a great way to grow in virtue, the culture surrounding sport can often make cultivating some of the virtues—like temperance, modesty, and humility—extremely difficult. In many ways professional sport leads the way in aggrandizing the vices of pride, anger, envy, sloth, greed, gluttony, and lust as its most prized icons. Vice, of course, is nothing new. It is the habit of doing bad and has been part of the human condition as far back as Adam and Eve. Today, however, the increasing competition for consumer dollars and attention, as well as advances in technology and communications, bombard us with every sordid detail. Nothing is held back. But as much as sport is a reflection of society it also has the ability to influence and shape it.

What can we do about it? Many good people tend to say one of two things: "Oh, well what can you do? I hate it. It's not right, but that's just the way it is." At the other end of the spectrum people say, "Well I just don't want anything to do with it. I refuse to even look at it." But I contend that neither approach is the right one.

Sport affects everyone. Even those who don't care about watching a major league baseball game can get caught in stadium traffic. Sport related products and activities generate *hundreds* of billions of dollars each year. The word "billion" gets thrown around like it's pocket change, but consider that if you stacked one billion single dollar bills on top of each other they would reach over sixty-three miles into space. That's a lot of cash to influence players and fans for good or for ill. To allow vice to dominate sport at all levels while thinking that it will not have an adverse impact on society and our culture, or that it's not going to negatively influence you, your children, or your grandchildren, is to live in denial; we criticize it, but we're actually enabling it to happen if we continue to support it and allow it to just keep rolling along in its present state.

The third option is for us—the fans, the coaches, the athletes, and the parents—to reclaim the game and take back sport, business, and everyday life by making them means for developing virtue. You can be a good person and a great performer both at the same time. They are not mutually exclusive. Sport, like everything we do, should be about the development of the whole person. Sport, then, can be used to impact society and culture for good, and it can be used to cultivate good and virtuous people, one athlete, coach, parent, or fan at a time. It can be quite difficult, but the good news is that many of the methods used to become a great athlete are the same methods used to become a virtuous person.

* * * * *

Too often we separate and compartmentalize our lives. We deal with the body over here, the mind over here, and the soul over here. Well, I don't know about you, but I'm all three things at the same fraction of a second. However helpful it may be to separate things in the order to talk or write about them, the reality is that we are all three things at the same time. Knowing how to make them all work together at the same moment is key to performing at the highest level and living a good life.

When I work with athletes, I go through the same process. In the first session I help them to improve some physical aspect of their game although they are usually unaware of how much it had to do with the mental and spiritual factors involved. The immediate positive result is a proof to them that there is something good happening here. Then I show them how their physical improvement is really rooted in their mental abilities and skills. And from there, they quickly come to see that both the physical and mental are mere extensions of their soul. All three are unified, connected.

Let me show you what I mean. A few years ago, I was working with a very talented NFL wide receiver. We were alone on an indoor turf field where I was throwing him passes at a high velocity while he ran various routes. After about seven or eight, he dropped a pass while running a ten yard out-pattern, and let slip a choice four-letter word while he stamped his foot down in disgust. "Whoa!" I said. He quickly looked over at me as the sound of my voice seemed to pull him back from his own little world. "What did you say?" I asked. He looked at me a little sheepishly and said, "Well, I, I dropped the ball." "I know you dropped the ball but what did you say?" I replied. "I was just upset that I dropped the ball," he shot back. "Thank you, Jesus," I said. He looked at me like I had hit him over the head with a two by four and said, "What do you mean?" This receiver is a Christian athlete, and so I asked him, "Aren't you thankful in all things?" (1 Th 5:18) He offered a hesitant "Y-y-y-yeah." So I repeated, "Thank you, Jesus." He paused for a second and then said, quite unenthusiastically, "Thank you, Jesus."

"Good, now come on back," I said.

There were two reasons why I encouraged him to say, "Thank you, Jesus." The first has to do with the virtue of gratitude: we should be thankful in all things. The second one is purely pragmatic and sports performance related. Can an NFL wide receiver catch a ball? Of course! So if he drops a ball it's certainly not because he can't catch. There's a reason he dropped the ball. The problem is that while he's cursing and stomping the ground in displeasure he has lost something: the awareness of *why* he dropped the ball. The reason for his anger was due to pride. He cursed to show me how upset he was about dropping the ball because *he* is much better than that and *he* doesn't drop balls. While he was doing that, however, he lost the precious moment when he had the ability to feel what happened. Unfortunately, since he didn't know why he dropped the ball, there's a good chance he would drop it again in the future for the same reason. But by saying, "Thank you, Jesus," he can immediately move past the emotions and reflect on what actually happened. Was the cut not sharp enough, did his head not snap around fast enough, did he not see the ball in detail, or did he not have energy in his hands greater than the ball?

He ran ten or twelve more routes, and eventually dropped another ball. He was about to say that word again but he caught himself and turned to look at me. I tilted my head slightly, and he said mechanically, "Thank you, Jesus."

"Good, now what happened?" I asked him. Although he wasn't absolutely sure, he thought that maybe he hadn't snapped his head around fast enough as he planted to make the out cut. He was right. Not surprisingly, he got better and better at knowing precisely what he did, and as a result he dropped fewer balls. Even he was amazed at some of the incredible catches that he made during the session, which in the past would have gone uncaught or written off as bad passes. Over time, this became natural, a good habit—a virtue. Now the first thing he says *if* he ever drops a ball is, "Thank you, Jesus!" and he means it.

In one session he improved in body, mind, and spirit and became not only a better wide receiver but a better person. This way of training and approaching life helped him to perform better physically. It helped him to focus his mind on the specific problems he was having catching the ball. And it helped him direct all his actions toward the good, toward God.

It's here where sport really shines. It not only holds the secrets to winning, of world-class and peak performances, but more importantly it can help you to become a better person physically, mentally, and spiritually. With dedication and a lot of practice, an athlete can make that last second shot, or that game-winning touchdown grab, and he can become virtuous. And the best part about sport is that he can do them both at the same time. All that is needed is desire and the willingness to act on it. Take the story you just heard. Chances are you're not an NFL wide receiver, but with gratitude, awareness, and focus on the task at hand, you will become a better husband, father, coach, or business professional. Once you know how sport is properly directed everything you do will be better.

That's the point of this book: to achieve peak performance—to be the best that you can be—on and off the field. Throughout I'll offer stories and exercises and drills that will not only help you become a better athlete, but, more importantly, will also help you become a better person. In my years of competing as an Olympic-level high jumper I've seen what it takes to achieve peak performance, and later as a sports psychologist, I've helped hundreds of professional and collegiate athletes become the best that they can be on and off the field. And I want to help you achieve the same success.

PART ONE

PREPARING YOUR MIND TO WIN

CHAPTER 1

ALL WORK AND NO PLAY

WHILE watching children play we are often struck by their total absorption in the present moment—*seriously sifting sand*—and their sheer spontaneous joy of the experience. One day I was teaching my son James to ride a bicycle. This may sound like a reasonably easy thing to do but as a father of ten children I always have something else going on around me. As I tried to stay focused on James, I heard one of his brothers yell, "Dad, look at me!" I looked over and another one shouted, "Heads up!" as a ball flew over us. In the middle of the melee I somehow became "base" for the group playing freeze tag. Now, just before I was pulled away by all of the commotion, James had his feet on the ground and was struggling to balance whenever he placed both of them on the pedals. Fortunately, every now and then there comes a special moment, a once in a lifetime experience when you are blessed to be in the right place at the right time and something wonderful occurs. Literally a second later, that moment would have passed unnoticed. At the exact instant when I turned back to look at James, he put his feet on both pedals and started to move. And this was the blessing: his face. I never witnessed such joy in someone's face as I did looking at James's in that moment. He was entirely unaware of me or anything else going on around him because he was completely absorbed in what he was doing, but I got to see that precise moment when he recognized that he was balancing and actually riding the bike. The joy was so intense that it felt like it physically shot out of him and hit me; it was extraordinary . . . and that's play. We tend to think that sport, unlike *child's* play, is more adult, work-like, and serious, when in fact just the opposite is true. We are attracted to sport because it is play!

The reason sport is so wildly popular is because every human being from the beginning of time has played. Yes, play. But for some reason most of us tend to think of play as something only little children like James do. Not so!

Johan Huizinga, in his 1938 book, *Homo Ludens* (*The Being that Plays*), analyzed the fundamental characteristics of play and the importance of its role in the very development of civilization. Roger Caillois, a French philosopher, built upon Huizinga's work and described six general characteristics of play in his book: *Man, Play and Games*. (1) Play is free, meaning it is not obligatory; you do not have to do it. Think back to a time when you couldn't wait to finish school or your chores so that you could play with your friends. Perhaps you can't even wait to get out to the golf course later today! (2) Play is separate since it has its own limits of space and time. Remember playing pick-up football on the street? Even spontaneous childhood games have boundaries: "The cars are out of bounds and the touchdown is past the stop sign. Game ends at five." (3) Play is uncertain because you do not know the outcome ahead of time. That is why a blowout is no fun to watch or play. You most enjoy a cliff-hanger especially when your team wins. (4) Play is unproductive since it basically ends like it begins. You brought a ball and you hopefully leave with a ball (unless you live in the Bronx and the football bounces into the street and gets sucked up under a car never to be seen again). (5) Play is governed by its own rules which are created for the moment: "Over the bush is an automatic home-run." (6) And finally, play is somewhat like make-believe. It is not "real" life but instead steps outside of it in a special way. Suddenly it's less than a minute to go, you are Johnny Unitas, Roger Staubach, Joe Montana or Drew Brees fading back to throw the winning Hail Mary, touchdown! That is play and like every other human who has ever lived, we have been doing it since our earliest childhood. This type of play, called *agon*, which translated from the Greek means competition, is the focus of this book. Sport is the competitive form of play.

Sport has been around for a long time. Robert G. Osterhoudt points out that sport's earliest practice coincided with humanity's earliest artistic and religious practices. Looking at a game like lacrosse, you can find its origin back as early as 4000 BC with the native Indian cultures of the New World. Track and field activities of the Proto-Celtic Europeans were embodied principally in the Tailteann Games of Ireland. These games began around 3000 BC. Nearly a thousand years later, the Proto-Greek Europeans began competing in track and field as well, and it is these games that were the precursors to the Olympic Games, which were first played in 776 BC.

Classical literature contains many references to sport and also describes how important it was to the life and culture of people from all places and in all times. These references suggest that sport and play were essential to the education and formation of youth. The list of those who have written about the importance and place of sport throughout history may surprise you. They are among the best and brightest that have ever lived.

The great philosopher Socrates (470–399 BC) was recorded as having said, "To have the body active and healthy can be hurtful to you in no occasions and since we cannot do anything without the body, it is certain that a good constitution will be of great advantage to us in all our undertakings. . . . And, indeed, it is shameful for a man to grow old before he has tried his own strength, and seen to what degree of dexterity of perfection he can attain, which he can never know if he give himself over for useless; because dexterity and strength come not of themselves, but by practice and exercise."

Later, Plato (428–348 BC), a student of Socrates, wrote, "For he who changes the sports is secretly changing the manners of the young, and making the old to be dishonored among them and the new to be honored." Aristotle (384–322 BC), a student of Plato, reinforced Socrates' claim of the importance of sport: "As in the Olympic Games it is not the most beautiful and the strongest that are crowned but those who compete (for it is some of these that are victorious), so those who act win, and rightly win, the noble and good things in life." The very fact that these luminaries of Western thought weighed in on sport reinforces the significance of play—of sport—as part of the human condition. Not surprisingly then, the multitude of saints and scholars who have also written about sport only deepens the intrigue about, and the importance of, sport in our time.

In 1896 the Olympic Games were resurrected for the first time since being discontinued in AD 393 by Emperor Theodosius, a Christian who had disapproved of the corrupt practices and professionalism which had begun to dominate sport. Baron Pierre de Coubertin, the father of the modern Olympics Games, sought to recapture all that was good in sport. The Olympic movement sought to link sport with culture and education, promote the practice of sport and the joy of effort, and help build a better world through sport practiced in a spirit of peace, excellence, friendship and respect (www.Olympic.org/Documents/Reports/EN/en_report_668.pdf).

In the tradition of Pindar, perhaps the greatest of the Greek lyrical poets who wrote victory odes for Olympic Champions, the Baron asked Kostas Palamus to write the Olympic Hymn which is still honored today.

> O ancient immortal spirit, pure Father of the true, the beautiful and the good, descend, appear, shed over us Thy light within the glory of your own earth and sky which has first witnessed Thy imperishable fame. Crown with the unfading branch, victors in the race and in strife! Create in our breasts, hearts of steel! In Thy light; plains, mountains and seas shine in a roseate hue and form a vast temple to which all nations throng to adore Thee, O ancient, immortal spirit.

These words, charged with religious references, describe the aspirational character he hoped would dominate the Games. The movie *Chariots of Fire* portrayed this character in its depiction of two great British runners who competed in the 1924 Paris Olympic Games: Eric Liddell, the 400m gold-medalist, and Harold Abrams, the 100m gold-medalist. One of the most striking scenes was when Eric Liddell refused to run in the Olympic 100 meters because the race was scheduled to take place on Sunday. While speaking to a crowd he said,

> You came to see a race today. To see someone win. It happened to be me. But I want you to do more than just watch a race. I want you to take part in it. I want to compare faith to running in a race. It's hard. It requires concentration of will, energy of soul. You experience elation when the winner breaks the tape—especially if you've got a bet on it! But how long does that last? You go home. Maybe your dinner's burnt. Maybe you haven't got a job. So who am I to say, "Believe, have faith," in the face of life's realities? I would like to give you something more permanent, but I can only point the way. I have no

formula for winning the race. Everyone runs in her own way, or his own way. And where does the power come from, to see the race to its end? From within. Jesus said, "Behold, the Kingdom of God is within you. If with all your hearts, you truly seek me, you shall ever surely find me." If you commit yourself to the love of Christ, then that is how you run a straight race.

There are two parallel plots in *Chariots of Fire*, one following Liddell and the other following Abrams. The latter chooses to focus exclusively on himself by obsessing over every situation and person in his life and how he will be perceived by them. And even after he won the gold-medal, it was interesting to observe that he could barely take it; he continued to struggle with an inner emptiness that no victory could fill. At one point he says, "I've known the fear of losing but now I am almost too frightened to win." His fear was that winning would not make him happy. He soon found out it was true. In stark contrast, Liddell, who ends up winning the 400m gold-medal, is just filled with pure joy. The difference is that Eric's life is centered on other people and how he could love them. He did that because God was the source and summit of his life. God was his center of gravity, his motivation, his inspiration, and challenged him to do the most he could with the skills, talents, and abilities with which he was blessed.

It didn't take long before the Olympic Games also became a platform for making grand political statements. In 1936 Adolf Hitler unsuccessfully tried to prove the superiority of the Arian race. In 1968, some U.S. athletes raised black gloved fists on the victor's podium as a statement about civil rights abuses. In the Munich Olympic Games members of the Israeli wrestling team were taken hostage and killed by Palestinian terrorists. The 1980 Moscow Games (I still have the letter from President Carter congratulating me on qualifying for the U.S. Olympic Trials and explaining why the United States would not be taking part in the Games) and the 1984 Los Angeles Games were boycotted by the United States and Soviet Union respectively. In Beijing, China attempted to show the world the perfection of Communism but in the end only proved that the individual was a commodity to be used by the state.

However, not all of the political posturing occurs within the Olympic arena. Well-known professional athletes often influence the public to endorse and vote for politicians and this has not gone unnoticed by the two major political parties in the United States. For example in the 2008 election, former Notre Dame quarterback Brady Quinn introduced Senator McCain at a rally and the NBA's Chauncey Billups did the same for Senator Obama. Consider all the politicians who were elected in part because of their athletic fame such as President George Bush; Vice-President Gerald Ford; Senators Jim Bunning and Bill Bradley; Congressmen Jack Kemp, Tom McMillan, Jim Ryun, Bob Mathias, Baron Hill, and Tom Osbourne; and Governor Arnold Schwarzenegger, to name just a few.

Although religion and politics may be closely associated with sport, in the end, it may be the economics of sport that has the greatest influence on our culture. The growth and sophistication of professional sport as a multi-billion dollar industry has only furthered the economic impact it has on every culture around the globe. For example, in 2011, New Zealand held the Rugby World Cup spending roughly $250 million to accommodate the event. It is estimated that the influx of 1.35 million tourists created well over 10,000 jobs and more than $320 million in the process. Writing for CNN, Doris Burke et al., asked, "Just how lucrative is the NFL? While the league won't divulge exactly how its $9.3 billion pie breaks down, that figure is slightly more than all of eBay's 2010 revenues and is roughly equivalent to the gross domestic product (GDP) of Macedonia." The Beijing Olympics provided that city with lasting revenue. The huge stadium built for the Games, the "Bird's Nest", has now become the third most visited monument in China after the Forbidden City and the Great Wall.

In 2010, the FIFA World Cup event generated $1.5 Billion in revenue and it is estimated that another $3 billion was spent on wagering. Revenue for the top-twenty soccer clubs is approximately $6 billion. After experiencing an economic crash, many in Britain hoped that hosting the 2012 Olympic Games in London would provide $2 billion in economic help they so desperately needed. World-wide advertising generates over $124 billion a year. Gambling generates another $144 billion. Consider that I have not listed the hundreds of billions of dollars generated by sporting goods manufacturers and retailers, food service providers, the internet, television, radio, print media, legal and medical services, and many more.

While the enormity of the sports industry often puts it in the limelight, it is important to remember what St. Francis de Sales, AD 1567–1622, of all people, had to say about the value and place of sport in our lives: "Games of skill, which exercise and strengthen body or mind, such as tennis, rackets, running at the ring, chess, and the like, are in themselves both lawful and good. Only one must avoid excess, either in the time given to them, or the amount of interest they absorb; for if too much time be given up to such things, they cease to be a recreation and become an occupation; and so far from resting and restoring mind or body, they have precisely the contrary effect."

Although we are surely *wired to* play, we are, first and foremost, *wired* for the truth. St. Francis may have written his words long ago but they are as true today as they were then. If we do not heed his wise counsel by enjoying sport for what it truly is, play, we will find ourselves drowning in the anti-religious, the political, and the economic morass that now pervades the world of sport. We will find ourselves working at sport rather than playing.

The steady diet of vice that we receive each day from the sports media would try to convince us that there is no apparent redeeming value to sport. That it is a pure den of iniquity. On the contrary, there are far more good things happening in sport than bad but we unfortunately hear precious little about them. During all the years I've spent among players, coaches, owners, and many others associated with sport, I've met and worked with incredibly gifted men and women who are models of professionalism, generosity, and virtue. In fact, they are exceptional men and women whom you would treasure as friends. They are loving husbands and wives, devoted fathers and mothers, and true men and women of faith.

The following stories are not rarities. They are among thousands that take place every year but rarely reach the light of day because the athletes involved did not lie, steal, cheat, or try to kill someone.

Amanda MacDonald apparently had had enough of the bad and was moved to write the following award-winning essay about an incident she witnessed during her brother's little league game.

> Ever since I can remember, I've played many sports—anything from T-ball to gymnastics; because of this, I've witnessed many acts of good sportsmanship, whether it was stopping to help an opponent in the middle of a cross county race, or a soccer player who helped a girl who fell while fighting for possession of a ball, or just a simple "Good game!" One example I've never forgotten took place during my little brother's 4th and 5th grade little league game.

It was a nice spring day. I was sitting unhappily in the old wooden bleachers at the dusty little league field behind our town's police station. Being in 6th grade at the time, I felt that I was way too cool to be watching this juvenile game of baseball, which my Mom had dragged me to. Little did I know that just one classy act performed by a 4th grade boy would influence my life. It was a long game, as most little league games tended to be. My brother's team was losing, even though they had the best pitcher in the league; he truly was an excellent pitcher, he threw better than most of the eighth graders at the time. It was probably the last inning and the team's coach let the little boy on the team who had cerebral palsy come up to bat. It took a lot of courage just for him to play, but to get up to bat was a whole other story, because he needed someone to run for him. When the little boy who was pitching saw this boy, he looked over to his coach as if to ask permission and walked about halfway between home plate and the pitcher's mound. He did this even as his team mates yelled, "Strike him out!" He lightly tossed the ball underhand to the batter until, on the third try, the boy with cerebral palsy got a hit and a runner on base. The pitcher did this despite the fact that his team was losing and it would have been an easy out; he did not cave in to the peer pressure his teammates put on him.

I know that everyone in the stands was amazed by the maturity of this boy's act and I know that when I look back at that moment I try to remember that if a ten-year-old boy can put aside his pride long enough to help someone feel good about themselves, I should be able to do the same. In today's world it is very difficult to stop being selfish and give to those who need our help.

I still know people, even grown-ups, who would not
have had the compassion to do what this little pitcher
did (Amanda MacDonald, "An Amazing Example of
Sportsmanship," www.miaa.net).

This story shows how works of mercy and virtue can touch
a life. That little guy who was pitching wasn't thinking, "Hey
I'm going to make a big statement here." He just did what he
believed was right, and you can see through his leadership—
which is really what he demonstrated—that his act has had an
impact.

This kind of virtuous behavior is not just for Little Leaguers,
either. Sara Tucholsky, a senior softball player for Western Ore-
gon University, was up to bat for the last time in her collegiate
career. At only 5' 2" she was not exactly a power hitter. Not only
had she never hit a home run in her life but of her thirty-four
at-bats that season she only had three hits. Sara found herself
at the plate in the top of the second inning with two runners
on base in a 0-0 tie with conference rival Central Washington
University. On the second pitch something happened that she
had dreamed about all of her life. Sara made solid contact, and
watched the ball sail beyond the field of play and over the out-
field fence for a home run. She was so elated that as she sprinted
past first base she missed touching the bag. Realizing it, she spun
around quickly to go back to touch it. Unfortunately her right
foot didn't go with her. As she pivoted, her cleats grabbed the
infield clay and she tore her anterior cruciate ligament in her
right knee. Immediately dropping to the ground with a loud yell
she laid there in pain unable to move.

No one was sure what to do next. The umpire told her
that if she did not make it around to all the bases she would
only be credited with a single. If any of her teammates helped
her she would be called out. Just then, Mallory Holtman, the

all-time conference home run hitter from the opposing team, approached the home plate umpire. She asked, "Could *we* pick her up and carry her around?" He stared back at her with a look of disbelief on his face, then consulted with the other umpires, and said, "Yes." Mallory and one of her teammates, Liz Wallace, approached Sara and asked her, "Would it be alright if we carried you around the bases?" Sara, somewhat overwhelmed, replied, "Yes! Thank you!" As they began to lift her up, Liz said, "You hit the ball over the fence and you deserve it."

Using a two-person arm carry, they slowly moved around the bases, gently touching her foot to each bag. As Mallory looked up into the stands as they rounded third heading for home, she realized that the entire crowd was on their feet clapping. Instead of cheering or yelling, she saw tears streaming down their faces. Everyone watching was overwhelmed with emotion by the act of love they had just witnessed. Tears of joy and gratitude were in Sara's eyes too. With her last time at bat, she had finally realized her life-long dream of hitting a home run.

What makes this even more memorable is the fact that these two teams were tied for the conference lead and were both desperate to win the championship title. Mallory and Liz may have helped Sara's team to win the game that day but their act of selflessness won the hearts of everyone who witnessed it.

TAKE AWAY

The joy of playing does not need to be sacrificed in the name of competition. On the contrary, the joy of playing includes winning and performing at your highest possible level. Sport asks for all of your mind, body and spirit to win the game. It also demands that it be done with virtue. Accepting anything less transforms play into a selfish work. It is no longer done for the higher purpose, for the contemplation of the highest things for their own sake, but rather for the base and fleeting ends of money, power and fame.

No matter how "big" sport may become, it is still play. Whether it's riding a bike for the first time, winning an Olympic gold medal, or becoming the next Superbowl MVP, sport is about the joy of competing and performing at your best. It challenges you and those you compete against to reach higher, to double your talents, to give back all that you have to give. And if it is motivated by virtue rather than an inordinate drive for money, power, or fame, then you will have in no small way moved one step closer to making peak performance a common occurrence in your life.

In the next four chapters we'll take a look at the things that can get in the way of play motivated by virtue and joy. We'll look at how they prevent peak performance. And we'll look at how you can overcome them.

CHAPTER 2

RUNNING ON EMPTY

YOU seem to have everything you could want but you're not really happy. Maybe you thought money, power, fame—*winning*—would make you happy. Why is winning so often anticlimactic? Why does the win fade so quickly and leave you feeling like you lost (or didn't win enough)? Why is it that some athletes can't walk away from the game? Why did Brett Favre, Sugar Ray Leonard, Roger Clemens, Manny Ramirez, and many other famous athletes desperately try to return after their first final goodbye? They're desperate for the approval or the love of others. Their reserves have run out and their tanks are empty. They need a refill.

Take school for example. Let's say that the first time you come home from school with a report card you have all D's. Mom and Dad look at it with real concern. Their vigilance increases and they check to make sure you're studying, and you are. You're working hard. They get you tutors, teach you study skills, the whole nine yards. You come home with your next report card and you *still* have all D's. Okay, this isn't good. They can see that you're working diligently, and they're doing everything that they can to help you. All of you redouble your efforts. Basically all they can say if you come home with more D's is, "Good job, keep working, keep trying."

On the other hand, imagine that you first come home with a report card with all A's. Everyone's excited. Mom and Dad continue to sing your praises and think, "My kid, the genius!" You start seeing the bumper stickers on the back of the van, "My Child Is An Honors Student." You get a huge clap on the back. This is great. But let's say at some point you come home with a C on your report card. You think that's going to go by unnoticed? No way. You're going to have to give an explanation. Something has changed. You realize that A's have become expected.

At this point you no longer get the same clap on the back for your good grades that you got the first time. This is not good, especially if you're doing it to get the clap on the back! But you're very adaptable. You become a juggler. You've got to try to maintain your A's, which by the way is taking a lot of effort. However, even the A's aren't earning you that clap on the back anymore, so with your left hand, you juggle the school stuff. You just keep that going. But you discover that you have a free hand! You're going to take on something new to get a much needed clap on the back: maybe it's athletics. Just like when you first started school, no one knows how you're going to perform. It turns out you've got talent. People are impressed. "You're fast! She's so strong. Look at his technique!" It's a big clap on the back, and it feels great. "Okay," you say, "I can do this." Now your juggling consists of keeping academics and athletics up in the air.

Soon, however, your high athletic performance also becomes expected. You don't get as big a clap on the back for a great play, because you're *supposed* to be that good. As a matter of fact, if you don't continually set personal bests people begin to wonder what's wrong with you. You're now expected to be a talented athlete. When this happens, you find another activity to add to your juggling act, looking for that clap on the back again. However, you only have 100 percent to give. Sometimes you will hear a coach say, "I wanna see you give me a 110 percent!" or you might say, "I gave it 110 percent." No, you didn't. There's no secret slice under the pie. You only have a hundred. At some point, you've taken on so many things in order to get a clap on the back that all 100 percent of your effort is tied up in juggling the things that have become expected, that you have to maintain. When you get to this point you begin to get a very strong feeling and usually it's a bad one. It might be anger, sadness, frustration, or depression—whatever it is, you're probably not going to like it.

What's happened is that being "good enough" has become tied to being loved. It may sound like a reach, but that's what it is. You're never going to say, "I'm doing this for love," but essentially that's just it. It's why we want the clap on the back, it's that love thing, and it's why we get upset when we don't have it.

This is something to be aware of in anything that you do. Are you doing it to show that you're "good enough"? Are you doing it for the love or approval of others? These, by the way, have nothing to do with each other. People who love you will continue to love you regardless of your performance. And what about those who don't seem to love you anymore when your performance suffers? Well, they never loved you from the start.

"Being good enough" is a powerful force that is always at work whether you are conscious of it or not. It is not a question of, "is it there," but rather to what degree does it affect your life, relationships, and the things that you do. What if I told you that the room you are sitting in no longer has any oxygen in it. You have to quickly find a way out. Otherwise you are going to die. You would do whatever it takes to get out; break a window, smash a wall, or scream for help. Now, what if I told you that instead of no oxygen in the room, there is no approval or love in the room? Well you may not like it but you're not going to die. When we make the mistake of equating the clap on the back with love, we make love like the oxygen. We absolutely have to have it or we feel like we are going to die. Every molecule of love becomes like the oxygen we need to live.

Think about what you are currently doing in order to be "good enough." What's really insidious about this is that often you will desperately try to get the love you crave from someone who can't give it to you. You're killing yourself to get it from a person who actually wasn't even capable of giving it to you in the first place. Why do you keep trying so hard? The reason you will not give up is because it *feels* like, "I need every drop of love I can get, I can't afford to lose one drop of it." Understanding to what degree this *drive* is present in your life and how to control it will free you up to perform better, enjoy what you are doing, and find the genuine love that may be eluding you now.

Sometimes the clap on the back can take other forms. Instead of performing to get it, many people will try to buy it. I have known and worked with many individuals who have made millions of dollars. On the face of it, this is not a problem. As a matter of fact it would seem like a very good thing. But only if you don't *need* it!

One major league baseball player I know was making about a million dollars a year. Due to a tax related issue, his income for the year was lower than usual and he would *only* be paid eight-hundred thousand dollars. I remember speaking with him at the time and he said to me, "I don't know what I am going to do this year. I am really strapped for cash." He was serious! Eight-hundred-thousand dollars! He sincerely felt that he would face hardships in the year to come because he would have to make do with a little more than three quarters of a million dollars. Now, I don't know about you, but when I hear eight-hundred thousand dollars I think, "Wow! How could he possibly think he would struggle or even have a difficult time with that kind of income?"

Before you judge him too harshly, think about your own life. Have you ever noticed a tendency to live up to your means?

Whether it's $35,000, $50,000, $100,000, or more than a million, we all tend to live on the edge of our incomes. It's easy to look at this player and rationalize about how he has a problem while we fail to see that we may be doing the same thing. The question you should be asking yourself is, "What am I buying and why am I buying it?" Your immediate response may be, "I needed it." But is that true? How often do you buy things that you really don't need? Probably more than you might like to admit. On occasion you may have found yourself buying things that you didn't even like too much. If so, you are not alone.

A very successful NFL player I worked with made millions of dollars, owned three Mercedes, two palatial homes, and could buy just about anything he wanted. When I first started working with him, I noticed that he would go out almost every day to the mall and buy a shirt. Yes, a shirt. Even though he was a Super Bowl champion, his tank was nearly empty. He was forever restless, distracted, and in need of a "fix." He used buying things as a temporary distraction and substitute to fill himself up until he could get his next big clap on the back. As you might imagine, it didn't work.

After bringing it to his attention and having many discussions about it, he was able to wean himself off buying things that he really did not need or want, and he began to focus on the things that could really fill him up. Once he started playing for the right reasons, he began to have fun again. He was shocked to find that he was also playing at a level that made his Super Bowl performances seem anemic. Playing like he was twelve again, for the sheer joy of it, began to fill his once perpetually empty tank.

Another reason the clap on the back can dominate your life is because your home, work, and social worlds tend to reinforce your need for it every day. One NFL player who I had worked with for many years fortunately came to this realization early in his career. He quickly learned that the NFL is about winning. It's a business and he would be "valued," not loved, by how well he performed. He would receive very little help from anyone and he would have to figure out how to survive and fit in quickly or he would be gone. They demanded that he meet their expectations, no excuses.

You may think that an NFL player, especially a young one, is continually being taught and coached. This is rare. There is a mentality that pervades which says, "You are the pro. We pay you a lot of money to perform. Go perform or get off the field." And if he isn't good enough there is a guy standing right behind him just dying for the opportunity to take his place. Of course there are exceptions but they are only temporary. You may see a first round draft pick who is a complete bust but the team seems to stick with him. That's because the person who drafted him does not want to admit they made a ten or twenty million dollar mistake. It's now a waiting game until his contract is up or they trade him to another team that hasn't fully realized the problem they would be inheriting.

For an example, look no further than the first round pick of the 2007 NFL draft, JaMarcus Russell. Guaranteed twenty-five million dollars, he was cut by the Oakland Raiders after only three years. Among the myriad of problems he faced, both from those around him and from himself, it is interesting to note the reason for his quick demise. He said, "I just got to where the game wasn't fun for me." He just couldn't figure out why his tank was empty. He didn't fully understand that the NFL is a business. It has nothing to do with fun or with him as a person. He is like any gladiator who entertains the crowd in violent contests with other gladiators, wild animals and condemned criminals. He will only survive for as long as he wins.

Those who do survive are usually busy filling their tanks. For many professional athletes the clap on the back comes in the form of big paychecks, public adulation, and the few seconds of fame captured on an ESPN highlight. College players transitioning to the pros struggle with this because their ready source of claps on the back expired upon leaving the stardom of their college teams. They were better than most of their college competition and mistakenly think life will be the same at the next level. They are wrong 99.9% of the time. They will now be playing exclusively with pro stars who, as veterans, are much faster, stronger, more skilled, mature, and fully adapted to the pro game.

To make matters worse, if new players have difficulty adjusting initially, even in small ways like an occasional dropped ball or missed assignment, they will be quickly labeled as not ready, or worse, a draft bust. And because they are rookies they will make mistakes. They will also find that no matter how desperate they may be for a clap on the back, few will be in the offing.

As if this isn't bad enough, they soon find that an error is not only a loss of the clap on the back, it is just the opposite of a clap on the back, and usually involves a public humiliation and tongue lashing by coaches or teammates. Each successive error is magnified and contributes to the next one, resulting in a downward spiral that seems to swallow the young player whole. Very soon the critical eyes that are ever present, constantly questioning a player's readiness or ability to play at the pro level, come to the conclusion, "No."

Since players are quickly assessed and labeled in the pros, their ability to let go of unnecessary baggage, including the need for claps on the back, is vital to their success. Jettisoning the old stuff makes room for learning the new things they will need in order to survive and thrive in the pros.

One wide receiver I worked with did this extraordinarily well. As a college star in one of the top football conferences in the country he was used to starting and playing the entire game. As an NFL rookie wide receiver, he would now need to come off the bench and step into a dramatically faster game with no opportunity to warm up. In his first game, I suggested that anytime the offense was on the field that he stand as close to the side-line as he was permitted. He should imagine that he was on the field playing, reading the defenses, watching how they move, feeling the intensity and speed of the game. He worked to generate the same energy as he would have had if he were standing on the line of scrimmage about to run a route. When the ball was thrown, he would see every detail of it from the time it left the QB's hand until it reached the hands of the receiver. By doing this on every offensive play, he felt like he had been actually on the field, playing in the game.

Eventually the moment arrived, late in the second quarter of his first professional game, on a third down play, his number was called. Because he didn't need the clap on the back, he wasn't worried about failing or dropping a pass. He was able to step onto the field, in the middle of a game, and make an exceptional catch and run for a first down. Those critical eyes that are always looking and judging saw this and said, "Oh yeah! He was a steal in the second round. We've gotta get him some more balls." Within a couple of games he was not only catching more passes, he had earned a starting position. He then went on to have a long and outstanding career. For him, being good enough and being loved had nothing to do with each other. He just enjoyed *playing* the game.

Your need for a clap on the back can often be hidden or disguised. For example, does it bother you when someone tells you your work is not good enough? Does it make you angry or defensive when someone criticizes your performance or informs you that you are not the right person for the job? You might be thinking, "What if they are wrong? Don't I have the right to be angry at someone who has unfairly judged me?" Okay let's say they are wrong, why all the emotion? On the other hand, what if they are right? Does it seem to especially hurt you when it comes from those you love and respect the most? If the answer is yes, then you might want to consider why it bothers you so much. After all, if their criticism is basically correct, what makes it so unpleasant to hear? The answer is fairly simple. The intensity of the hurt or anger you experience when told that you do not measure up in some way will be proportional to the intensity of your need for each drop of love.

It might explain the outrageous behavior of so many athletes who completely lose control of their emotions during competition. In the 2009 U.S Open, for example, women's tennis star Serena Williams lost control of her emotions on the way to losing the semi-final match with Kim Clijsters, the eventual overall champion. After the first set, Serena had received a warning and a fine for smashing her racquet. Towards the end of the match, she was called by the line-judge for a foot fault on her serve. This moved her to within one point of losing the match. Although she is a very talented player and might have worked her way out of this desperate situation, she instead stepped toward the official with racquet raised and reportedly screaming, "I swear to God I'm [expletive] going to take this [expletive] ball and shove it down your [expletive] throat, you hear that? I swear to God." The line-judge was called over to the chair umpire to report what was going on. The line-judge then returned to her seat, and Serena pointed and began walking toward her. The line-judge then headed back towards the chair umpire. Tournament referee Brian Earley walked onto the court at the same time to assess the situation. He could be heard asking the line-judge what Serena said. Serena then walked over to join the conference. Towering over the line-judge she said, "Are you scared? Because I said I would hit you? I'm sorry, but there's a lot of people who've said way worse."

This eventually resulted in her losing an additional point

since she had already received a warning for smashing her racquet. "What she did was unacceptable. It's unacceptable behavior under any circumstances. When you're on the court, and you are waving your racket toward a lines-person and using profanity, it's just simply unacceptable," said Tournament Director Jim Curley. "When you look at the tape, it's pretty clear that the way she approached the lines-person, with her racket and in that manner, it was a threatening manner. It certainly was."

Serena did release a statement through a public relations firm, acknowledging that "in the heat of battle I let my passion and emotion get the better of me and as a result handled the situation poorly." Were passion and emotion some outside force beyond her control? For her they were since she did not apologize for the outburst. When asked about it she said, "An apology from me? How many people yell at lines-people? I see it happening all the time. I don't know how many times I have seen that happen. I am a professional. I'm not the beggar, like, 'Please, please, please, let me have another chance.'"

It was also interesting to hear more rationalizations from former tennis star John McEnroe who was notorious for his angry outbursts on the court. He said, "In my opinion, you can't call a foot fault there. Just out of the question. Can't do it. It was so close. Not as if it was an obvious foot fault—it was minuscule. I've seen Serena come back from that position a dozen times against top-flight opponents. The match was not over." John justifies her behavior because he believes that the line judge should not have made the call because the point was *too* important. Really? Me, me, me. It is all about me. It has to be since they are so desperate for a clap on the back. And, apparently, they will do and say whatever it takes to get one.

When it was all over, Serena was fined the maximum on-site penalty of $10,000 for the infraction and later received a record fine of $82,500 from the Grand Slam Tournament Committee.

Given her $350,000 U.S. Open prize money and her $6.5 million annual earnings that year, it was not excessive. The one thing a fine could not do, however, was give Kim Clijsters the joy of experiencing the winning point.

Could all of this have been avoided? Yes. If you think not, just imagine behaving like Serena Williams at work or with your family. This type of behavior would ensure that you remain unemployed and probably destroy every relationship in your life. Hopefully this way of responding to challenging situations is unacceptable to you. So why would anyone think that it should be acceptable in sport? In terms of physical performance, anger might enable you to muster enough strength to overcome an assailant in a desperate situation but it rarely works with activities that require precision and control. Players like Williams, McEnroe, and others are so talented that they often win in spite of their anger rather than because of it. For Serena, her behavior was certainly one sign of a tank in need of filling. It seems ironic that the anger exhibited in response to losing facilitated the very thing she hoped to avoid, losing.

When you spend most of your time as an athlete trying to get a clap on the back you get tired, very tired. Day after day, month after month, year after year, feeling driven to perform and not recognizing why. This feeling of being "burned-out" can happen to any of us. We'll use that phrase, "burned-out," to describe how we feel when we have nothing left in our tanks or when we can't go on at the pace required to keep them filled up. Usually about this time we cry out, "I need a vacation." Funny how the rest we seek is often more full of activity than the life we were supposedly retreating from. Upon returning, we often moan, "I am exhausted. I need a vacation from my vacation." So how do we get one and what can we do about this life that seems to be rolling along at break-neck speed?

One thing to realize is that getting burned-out is basically caused by two things. First, you can be genuinely physically and mentally exhausted; even if you love what you are doing, you can still get exhausted doing it. Some of the symptoms of over-training or overworking include an ongoing feeling of perpetual fatigue, getting sick more easily and frequently, loss of appetite, and sometimes difficulty falling asleep or staying asleep even when you feel very tired. The second, however, is more subtle and, like an iceberg that conceals 90 percent of its mass below the surface, it can be a great danger to the unwary. You may experience a strong sense of dissatisfaction or ineffectiveness with what you've been doing. It is no longer rewarding. You no longer enjoy doing it and if left unchecked, you may even experience feelings of helplessness, hopelessness, or depression. The symptoms of this second kind of burn-out are like the tip of an iceberg because they do not reveal the true cause of the problem.

The solution to the first cause is fairly straight forward. Just like an athlete, changing some aspect of your work such as the type, intensity, frequency, or duration, as well as ensuring a good diet, will often resolve the feeling of fatigue fairly quickly.

The solution to the second kind of burn-out comes with understanding what is driving you to work and perform. If almost everything you do is for a clap on the back then you will eventually burn-out.

For example, look at a relationship where one person is constantly giving and the other is constantly taking. At first blush this looks like it might work. Isn't everyone happy doing what they like to do best, giving and taking? If the person who is giving is doing so because they choose to do so, no problem. However, if the giver is consciously or unconsciously doing it to get a clap on the back, some love, then there will be a big problem sooner or later. At some point, a day from now or several years from now, the giver is going to say, "Just a little bit." The taker will look with a blank stare and say, "A little what?" "Just a little love, not much, just a touch," says the giver. The taker then says, "Whoa, wait a minute. The deal was you were going to love me and I was going to let you." At this point the giver is shocked to find that the person being asked for a little love is incapable of giving any. The symptoms of burn-out, if not already present, are well on their way.

A young NBA player that I had begun working with called me one afternoon and said he wanted to get together to discuss something of importance with me. For the sake of anonymity I will call him Chris. I asked if he wanted to discuss it over the phone but he felt it was important enough that it needed to be in-person. I asked him what it was about so that I could prepare for our meeting but he said he would rather wait until we were together to talk about it. Although I had only just started working with Chris a couple of weeks earlier, I thought it must be something personal because we had already discussed important issues and decisions related to his game performance by phone.

However, as we sat down in his home the next day, I was surprised to hear him say, "I think I want to quit." I could see it in his eyes, he was feeling down. He wanted to discuss this with someone who he thought would be objective and direct him in how to make the right decision. Chris thought he wanted to quit but he was worried about how it would affect everyone in his life. He was tired, injured, didn't like his coach, and no longer enjoyed the game. He especially did not like the off-court attention that he described as, "Smothering me." How could he tell his family and the world that he hated playing basketball? Only twenty-five years old and on his way to being burned-out.

Chris had a strong need for claps on the back but as a pro he found they were not enough. No matter how hard he tried to prove himself, no one in the organization seemed to pay him much attention. There were requests for interviews and sponsorship offers but it was clear to him that he was just an interchangeable cog in the money-making machine of sport. No one really cared about him one way or the other. He was smart enough to see through the hype and realized that the guaranteed money, fame and access he enjoyed never seemed to fill him up.

I told him about an insight I had while staying in Las Vegas of all places.

As I was preparing for a presentation that I would be making I looked out the hotel room window. Not being a high roller my room overlooked the decaying top of the casino below. The roof was old, dirty and falling apart and the backs of the electrical signs were filthy and rusted. My unique vantage point allowed me to simultaneously see both the bright flashing lights on one side of the strip and the ugliness of the casino roof and rust on the other. It seemed so clear to me that all the glitter and gold on the surface was in reality a shallow veneer covering the dirt and decay within. He lit up and said, "Yeah, that's it. That's my life!"

He was a quick study and after about three hours of discussing the source of his need for claps on the back, he came to the conclusion that he still really enjoyed basketball but he had stopped *playing* the game. Over the next few months, I continued to challenge Chris to think about why he was doing the things that he did and how, if at all, they affected those he worked with and loved. With some time off he rehabbed, worked on his relationships, and returned the next season with a different attitude and perspective, and best of all, he was excited to play.

Unfortunately, more often than not, athletes do not recognize the trap they have fallen into and, despite their "brand" image, they will often struggle either on or off the court, or sometimes both. Most of the athletes that I have worked with over the years avoided these problems because they were able to keep everything that was happening to them in proper perspective. They weren't looking for a clap on the back and they certainly didn't need one.

How you see things and interpret what they mean has a lot to do with your happiness and success in life. The physical, mental, and spiritual formation you received growing up prepares you to respond well to the challenges of life. This formation is not the kind that can be administered in small doses. It demands a full and continuous immersion in order to create the enduring character that makes you, *you*. Sometimes through no fault of your own, you may have had a difficult home life while growing up and not received the kind of love and formation that would have better prepared you for your life today, but it's not too late. More challenging perhaps, but definitely not too late. The individuals you will soon read about, as well as each ensuing chapter, will provide the insights and answers that will help you fill your tank and keep it full.

The following story describes an athlete whose formation prepared him to respond well. He was free to perform at his best in any given situation and, as you will see, he did. The decision he made in a split second, under pressure, was the result of years of training in virtue that had prepared him to make the right choices in the blink of an eye. He was not self-absorbed and he did not need a clap on the back or the world's approval to feel good. His actions, in the heat of battle, had a lasting impact on his life well beyond anything that he could have ever thought or imagined at the time. You are no different. You are faced with challenges and difficult decisions every day of your life. The question is, "How will you respond?"

Perhaps one of the finest athletes who ever competed in any sport was Australian miler John Landy. He ran for the pure joy and challenge of trying to be the first man to break the four minute mile barrier. If there was ever an athlete who embodied the spirit of excellence and virtue in all that he did, it was John. There were two other men on the same quest but they were running for less inspired reasons. Roger Bannister of Great Britain ran for the glory of being the first man to cover the mile in a time that experts thought impossible and Wes Santi of the United States ran to escape an abusive home life. The three traded world records back and forth in rapid succession, each inching ever closer to the four minute citadel. People from every nation were riveted to their radios and newspapers hoping to learn that the walls had been breached. At that time, there were no 24/7 news outlets or sports programs like ESPN beaming their signals around the globe. So it is not surprising that the incredible performances of these three young men had captivated the world's attention. And they did not disappoint. The first sub-four minute mile was finally achieved by Roger Bannister on May 6, 1954 in a time of 3:59.4. Remarkably, the four minute barrier, which had seemed for so long beyond human reach, was broken for the second time just forty-six days later on June 21st in Turku, Finland by John Landy with a time of 3:57.9, which the IAAF ratified as 3:58.0 due to the rounding rules then in effect. Although Roger Bannister was the first to run under four minutes for the mile, there was something exceptional about John Landy the man.

Volumes could be written to describe the extraordinary character of John Landy but the following story and letter captures all you need to know about him. The 1956 Australian National Championships served as the venue for one the most memorable acts of sportsmanship in Track and Field history and perhaps in all of sport. At the time, John Landy was the world record holder in the mile run and a favorite to win at the Australian National Championships. The Melbourne Olympic Park was filled to capacity. The crowd was electrified as they awaited the much anticipated mile run. They wanted to be part of something special, history in the making. They knew the record could be broken and that John Landy, a son of Melbourne, was the man to do it. At the start of the race, there was a lot of jostling for position. The first lap went well and was run in 59.0 seconds, just under world record pace. Robbie Morgan-Morris was in first followed by Ron Clarke, Alec Henderson, John Plummer, and then John Landy. An eyewitness of the race, the Rev. Dr. Gordon Moyes, wrote:

> Then occurred an event which is etched into my mind so clearly that I can see it being replayed as if in slow motion. I can never think of the event without my eyes filling with tears. Clarke was moving to the lead as they came into the corner on the third lap. John Landy was on his shoulder. Alec Henderson tried to squeeze between the two runners and the inside edge of the curb. In doing so Clarke, with his spikes, clipped his heel. Clarke sprawled forward onto the cinder track while Henderson was knocked onto the infield. Landy leaped over the falling body of Clarke in front of him and as he did his sharp spikes tore into the flesh of Clarke's shoulder. The whole field either jumped over Clarke or ran round him. The crowd which had been chanting "Landy, Landy, Landy, Landy" with every stride suddenly responded with an enormous gasp. Landy then did the most incredibly stupid, beautiful, foolish, gentlemanly act I have ever seen. He stopped, ran back to the fallen young Ron Clarke and helped him up to his feet, brushed cinders from knees and checking his bloodied shoulder said "Sorry." Clarke was all right. He said to Landy "Keep going, I'm all right. Run! Run!" Landy had forgotten everything. The Australian mile title, his bid for a world record, even the approaching Olympic Games, in a spontaneous gesture of sportsmanship.

Landy was now forty or fifty yards behind the leader. After having come to a complete stop it was remarkable to see how quickly he was able to accelerate up the home straightaway. One by one he picked them off. The roar of the crowd was deafening as he passed the race leader off the final turn and, with winged feet, flew down the home stretch breaking the tape in a time of 4:04.2. Rather than immediately celebrating his remarkable come-from-behind win, he turned to welcome Clarke across the finish line and to check on his injury. It is difficult to know exactly how much time was lost in Landy's spontaneous act of selflessness but some say as much as fifteen seconds, others no more than seven. What is universally agreed upon is that had he not stopped and gone back to help Clarke up, he would have broken the world record. After much urging, Landy reluctantly began a victory lap. As he circled the track the applause would not die. It seemed to go on forever and, in a certain sense, it did. To this day many people believe that it was the greatest mile ever run.

In June of 2002 a bronze sculpture, immortalizing John Landy's act of sportsmanship during the 1956 Australian National Championships and a letter by sports journalist Harry Gordon, was placed outside of Melbourne's Olympic Park.

Dear John,

The fellows in the Press box don't have many heroes. Often they help make them—usually they know too much about them to believe in them. Up in the Press seats they don't usually clap. They are busy and they are used to big sport. Mostly they've mastered the art of observing without becoming excited. On Saturday, at 4:35, the sports writers forgot the rules. They had a hero . . . every one of them. And you were it. Among the 22,000 who crammed into Olympic Park, there was not a soul who was not thrilled and inspired by your effort. None of them will forget it. Yours was the classic sporting gesture. It was a senseless piece of chivalry—but it will be remembered as one of the finest actions in the history of sport. In a nutshell, you sacrificed the chance of a world record to go to the aid of a fallen rival. And in pulling up, trotting back to Ron Clarke, muttering "Sorry" and deciding to chase the field, you achieved much more than any world record. Your action cost you six to seven seconds. And you sprinted round that last lap like a 220 runner and you overhauled the field to win in 4 minutes 4.2 seconds. You . . . the fellow who used to be called a mechanical runner without a finish! A lot of people are wondering why you pulled up. The truth is, of course, that you didn't think about it. It was the instinctive action of a man whose mate is in trouble. In the record books it will look like a very ordinary run for these days. But, for my money, the fantastic gesture and the valiant recovery make it overshadow your magnificent miles in Turku (3:58.0 WR) and Vancouver (3:59.6, second to Roger Bannister's 3:58.8). It is your greatest triumph. And it is fitting that it took place in your home town (Harry Gordon, 2004).

Typical of his humility, Landy, upon seeing the sculpture said, "While Lot's wife was turned into a pillar of salt for looking back, I'm probably the only one ever turned into bronze for looking back."

TAKE AWAY

Landy made virtue a way of life. He wasn't perfect but he tried to achieve it every day, in every way possible. He didn't need the praise of others to feel good about himself but instead chose to work conscientiously by placing love of duty above his inclinations without ever shrinking from it through weariness or difficulty of work. Certainly he had exceptional physical and technical abilities but what set him apart from every other world-class athlete is something that you are capable of possessing. You are called to live and practice the same heroic virtue in your life that Landy lived in his.

Keep in mind, being "good enough" has nothing to do with being loved. Knowing this removes the anxieties and worries that can hurt your performance and prevent you from using all of the skills, talents and abilities with which you have been blessed. The freedom to excel in whatever you choose to do in life will only come when you are able to separate the two. Remember that no clap on the back, no matter how big or how frequent, will ever fully satisfy you. The following chapters will reveal more and more about what it takes to fill your tank, achieve heroic virtue, and perform at your very best.

CHAPTER 3

UNSPORTSMANLIKE CONDUCT

YOUR team just made a great defensive stop on third and three with time running out and the lead. Hold on! There was a flag on the play. All you hear after the play is, "personal foul, unsportsmanlike conduct, fifteen yard penalty, automatic first down." Your team then goes on to lose the game. What was going on inside the head of the player who committed the foul? Why would he have done something that was so obviously hurtful to your team and the outcome of the game? He certainly did not want to lose the game but his angry outburst did just that. What caused him to *feel* so angry? What did he *believe* was happening? The answer to these questions may explain why the meek will not only inherit the earth but will also win the game.

Imagine for a moment that you and I are working on a project and a third person joins us. After the brief introductions, you ask the person who joined us to read page eight of the instruction manual so we can begin our work. He says, "Well . . . okay but what are we doing?" Again, very politely, you ask him, "Please read page eight." He says, "Okay but what are we doing?" And once again you very kindly ask him to please read page eight. Instead of doing what you asked him to do, he begins to get pretty agitated and seems to be questioning your authority.

Before long, an argument ensues. This person is really angry, so fired up, in fact, that he starts yelling and screaming at you, and throws the book at you. What's your first thought about this person? Most people would say that he's a real jerk. It's understandable how somebody might come to that conclusion.

But what if I told you now that that man can't read? "Ohhhh, I didn't know . . ." It's interesting to see how quickly emotions can change. When you assumed this person could read and then he acted in this inappropriate way, yelling, screaming, throwing the book at you, you get angry, you get ticked-off. Now, two seconds later, you feel differently about him. "He can't read! I didn't *know* that." It's like a switch was flicked in your head and suddenly you have empathy for the man. Anger and empathy are at opposite ends of the spectrum. Even though we agree that it is unacceptable to yell, scream and throw things at people, you are now willing to give him every break in the world because you think, "I know he's wrong for what he did but he may have been too embarrassed or humiliated to tell me about it." Your emotions rushed from one end of the spectrum, anger, to the opposite, empathy, in an instant. Emotions are powerful and often seem unchangeable but in reality they are based on what you *believe.*

This is an important insight for relating to people in your life who are difficult to deal with, even when they are being nasty or obnoxious. They're the kind of people whom you try to get away from. You may think, "They just like being that way." Well, wait a second. Consider that the most motivating thing to any human being is love. Somebody who is doing something that makes you want to push them away or get away from them means that they're not getting the thing they want most: your love. It's what they want most of all, so it seems kind of crazy that they do things to push you away. It's a downward spiral for them, as they keep doing these abrasive things over and over, making it that much more unpleasant to be around them, they get less and less of the thing they want most, love.

Go back to the example of the illiterate man. Think of reading as a skill much like any other you might have such as your ability to communicate or love. You are going to encounter people who can't *read* or can't communicate or can't love well. Instead of assuming that they can *read* and becoming frustrated with them, try to hold your judgment and determine if in fact they can *read*. If you come to discover that they can't *read* you will avoid getting upset, hurt, or drawn into a fight because understanding the person will usually lead you to empathy.

You might be tempted to ask, "How do I know that it's the other person that can't *read* and not me?" Here's a little test you can take. Ask yourself, "Do I want to be in this person's shoes?" If you're dealing with one of these unhappy people described above your immediate answer will be, "No! I wouldn't want to be in their shoes." Why? Because you think, "I'd be miserable. My life may have its difficulties but they aren't that bad." You might also be tempted to think, "But they seem to like it. They even have an attitude about it and they don't seem very sorry to be this way." So this person, who wants to love, is doing these things that drive love away and is *really* enjoying himself?

Imagine for a moment that we're in a bowling alley. The guy in the next lane picks up a ball and drops it on his foot. Then he picks up the ball and drops it on his foot again. And again. You are not going to turn to me and say, "Hey, the guy over there in lane two is having a great time." You're going to say, "There is something terribly *wrong* with that man." It doesn't matter how he reacts either. No matter whether he's screaming in pain, smiling, or laughing, you're not going to say, "He must be happy." There is a problem because clearly this person is hurting himself. Anyone who keeps dropping a bowling ball on their foot has a problem. Likewise, whether they seem to enjoy it or not, these people who are angry, obnoxious, or generally unpleasant to be around, are hurting themselves. They are dropping bowling balls on their feet with every offensive word or action. They are missing out on the one thing they want most: love. And they are doing it to themselves by driving people away. If we can recognize that in people, it will do two things. It will help us love that person more, to be empathetic, and to realize that they have a problem. It will also help us not to get wrapped up in reacting with emotions that we don't really want to experience and that will end up hurting us and those we love.

Sometimes, though, we are the ones who can't *read* and we may cut off relationships or lose opportunities because of our assumptions and rash judgments. Often this happens due to a lack of awareness and vigilance in seeking out and confirming what is true in our everyday lives.

Once, when I was working as a sports psychologist, a man by the name of Bob called me about his golf game and told me that he was depressed. He told me that he usually shot two or three over par but that his game had slowly deteriorated and he was feeling miserable and depressed. I told him we should meet in-person so that I could evaluate not only how he was thinking but also determine if there were any physical issues that might be contributing to his problem. When he arrived at the clinic I was taken aback to see that he was only about 5'2". It was also obvious that he had a distinct limp. "Nothing wrong with being 5'2" and having a limp but a near scratch golfer? I don't think so," I thought. During the exam I asked him, "Do you have any injuries? Back problems?" "No", he said, "but I do have a leg length discrepancy." It turned out to be a very significant discrepancy: about two inches. I thought, "Wow, just imagine what his swing must look like." However, Bob had told me over the phone that he was almost a scratch golfer, meaning he shot near par pretty consistently. When asked again about his score, he said, "Yeah, I have always played pretty well. I have been a one or two handicap since I was in my twenties." Taking him at his word, at least until I saw him play, I concluded that his physical limitations must not be the problem. It had to be something else. So I said to him, "Well, let's go out to the course and let me watch you play a few holes so I can get a sense of what you're doing."

As soon as we arrived at his course, he jumped out of the car, grabbed his clubs and practically ran to the pro shop. He jumped into one side of a cart and I had to quickly leap into the other in order not to be left behind. We arrived at the first hole without a warm-up. He stepped out of the cart and before I knew what was happening, he grabbed his club, walked up to the ball, no warm-up swing or anything, and hit it without hesitation. This was like extreme golf where players run from hole to hole and play as quickly as possible. His swing was a bizarre gyration of blurred movements that couldn't possibly make contact with the ball but amazingly his ball flew about two-hundred and fifty yards down the middle of the fairway. Being a professional, I tried to discretely lift my jaw off the ground and conceal my utter astonishment. We jumped back in the cart like Navy Seals on a mission and sped off to rescue his ball. We skidded to a stop, he leapt out, and before I had time to look up, he had picked out the appropriate club, a 7 iron this time, walked right up to the ball, no practice swing or delay, and hit another beautiful shot, dead center, this time about fifty yards short of the green. I hoped at this point that he thought my jaw was always on the ground.

Then, on the next shot something happened. He changed. Bob slowed down, debated with himself about which club to choose, and readjusted his grip three or four times before finally taking a slow and measured swing. His ball flew over the green about twenty yards left of the hole. By now it was evident to me that Bob did not have a problem with depression; he was really only feeling upset about his game after not playing as well as he normally did. He also didn't have a problem due to his unusual physical attributes. The reason he wasn't playing at his best? One day about a year earlier he had been playing with someone who caused him to slow down on his short approach shots. Because of this he had hit several shots like the one I described above. Normally this might not be a problem for most people but Bob was the type of player who just played and did not think about what he was doing. His strength had been in not being overly analytical while playing. This type of player usually plays well and, to the chagrin of those more analytically inclined who play with him, seems not to have a care in the world. However, the Achilles heel of this player is exposed when he begins to play poorly. He is usually unaware of how he makes his good shot and therefore does not know how to adjust it when it falls apart. In Bob's case he began changing one thing and then another, and another. Soon he had begun to switch to new clubs, grips, balls, gloves, techniques, with ever worsening results. He had not recognized what he was doing and then finally one day he woke up "depressed." The solution for Bob was remarkably simple, go back to playing the way he always played: fast! I spoke to him for a few minutes about this and then I dropped another ball down where he had hit the previous short shot. I had him quickly walk up to the ball, and with no practice swing or grip adjustments, hit it. The ball sailed high and landed about fifteen feet from the hole. He turned to me with a look of joy, excitement and disbelief. Bob was back! By the end of the round he was striking every ball with consistency and accuracy. It didn't take him long to return to his one or two handicap which made him very happy and not the least bit depressed. The reason this story turned out so well was because I didn't allow my first impressions to bias my assessment of Bob and his ability to play golf. I had learned this lesson years earlier from a young guy by the name of Daniel.

When I was coaching at Boston University, I had one of the best high jumping squads in the country. Nick Saunders was an NCAA Division I National Champion who had also won the Commonwealth Games, placed fifth in the 1988 Olympic Games, and had a career best jump of 7'9". His 7'9" jump remains a Commonwealth Games record and is one of the highest jumps in history. Another member of the squad, Greg Gonsalves, was an NCAA Division I All-American who had a personal best jump of 7'5". There were two other men jumping around the 7'0" level and one or two just shy of it. The women's squad was also outstanding. Julie White had a personal best of 6'2" and, as a sixteen year old, jumped 6'1" in the 1976 Olympic Games to place tenth. There were two other women who had jumped close to 6'0". It was just an incredible group of athletes.

It was the beginning of the school year when I first met Daniel. We were out on the field at Boston University preparing to begin a technique session. The mats, standards, and high jump bar were ready to go. The women were going to jump first and as they were taking some warm-up jumps, this young guy comes over to me full of enthusiasm and says, "Hi Coach! My name's Daniel and I'm a new freshman. I'd really like to be on the track team and I'd like to high jump. I'm a high jumper." Now I had more jumpers than I knew what to do with, but despite his physical stature, which looked nothing like a high jumper, I thought, "You never know, he could be the next world record holder." I told him the women were warming up at the moment but that I'd like to see him take a jump. Because the women were jumping at the time, the bar was only set at 5'4". It did not matter that the bar was too low because as soon as I see an athlete move I can get an accurate sense about the individual's current ability and future potential. I watched as he rocked back and forth and then began his approach. He went up on his first jump and nearly took the bar off with his head. Everyone's eyes went wide and their mouths hung open. He ran back to me, apologized breathlessly and looked frustrated with himself. "Please let me take another," he said. On his second jump he nearly broke the bar by landing on it with his back. The jumpers gathered around me and they started talking about him, "Coach, get rid of this guy, he's a loser. He can't even get over five four." I quickly responded, "Hey now, none of that. Move on." So they all dispersed. Meanwhile, Daniel ran back over to me, and by then he was really flustered and upset. "I don't know what's wrong, I'm just a little off today," he said. But I can see that he's just not built like a high jumper at all, he's five feet ten inches tall, weighs about a hundred and eighty-five pounds, his elbows are out, his knees are in; he doesn't even look like an athlete to me. I asked him some questions and I found out he was in general studies and that school was a challenge for him. This would probably mean a lot to him. So I said to him, "Okay, I'll tell you what, if you come out every day, you listen to me and do what I tell you, you can be on the team." "Ohhh! Thank you so much!" and he ran off excited as can be. Now you might be thinking, "Awww, that was really nice of you." However, I learned an incredible lesson from Daniel. To make a long story short, by the end of his senior year, Daniel jumped seven feet one inches! To put this in some perspective, jumping seven feet is like breaking the four minute mile. Daniel, who I thought would have difficulty ever clearing six feet, jumped over seven feet. I learned something from Daniel that has stayed with me to this very day: never underestimate anyone. In high jumping, the seven foot barrier is something every high jumper aspires to break, and Daniel broke it. Too often we underestimate people and write them off too quickly. You may tend to write yourself off too easily as well, when in fact, as you will learn in chapters six and seven, you are capable of incredible feats of strength, skill and focus.

You may think that the pros are different. They have it all together. They are not like you. They don't need to do a thing except show up and play. The truth is that I have never worked with a professional athlete who didn't have further to go than he had already come. Wes Welker, whose name has become synonymous with superstar, is one of the most striking examples of this. He is an exceptional athlete who always seems to make the play when his team needs it the most. He is a highly successful NFL wide receiver, but it wasn't always that way. His story is a great lesson for those of us who perhaps unwittingly underestimate ourselves or others.

Wes played exceptionally well at Heritage Hall H.S. in Oklahoma City and like most talented high school players he had dreams of playing in college. Unfortunately for Wes no college or university seemed to be very interested. As a matter of fact, his high school coach tried desperately to get someone, anyone, interested in his star player. He sent out over a hundred faxes to college coaches around the country hoping to find just one who might have a roster spot for Wes. Not one bite! In the eleventh hour, the coach from Texas Tech called to say that one of his recruits had backed out and he had one scholarship available if Wes was still interested. Wes jumped at the opportunity. Although he went on to have a prolific career at Texas Tech which included an NCAA record for punt return touchdowns (8) and the Mosi Tatupu Award in his senior year (an award given to the best special teams player in the country), he was not invited to the 2004 NFL combine. As a 5'9" wide receiver who ran a slow 4.55 second 40-yard dash, Wes was not considered NFL material by the scouts. Somehow, he managed to sign as a free agent with the San Diego Chargers and was invited to training camp, but they released him before the season began.

I have seen this happen with a number of players that I

have worked with in the past. A player is labeled before he even shows up at camp and it is almost impossible to get a team to change its perspective about him no matter how well he performs. I have seen a rookie free agent out-perform veterans and high draft picks and still not make the team. Typically the player is not given the chance to overcome the label and prove that he should be playing. When he is released by the team, coaches say in a self fulfilling prophecy, "See, I knew he was too small, too slow, too . . ." Later, Charger's Coach Marty Schottenheimer would say of releasing Welker, "It was the biggest mistake we ever made!"

Despite all the setbacks, Wes's perseverance and hard work eventually paid off. He signed with the Miami Dolphins and when finally given the chance, he played very well. Fortunately for him he had particularly good games against their conference rival the New England Patriots. Whether they saw his true talent or just wanted to remove a player who gave them fits every time they met, the Patriots traded two draft picks to the Dolphins for Wes in 2007. From there his career skyrocketed. Given the opportunity to show what he was capable of doing, Wes went on to set many Patriots' franchise records and seven NFL all-time records as well as accumulating thousands of all-purpose yards and more. This is from the guy who was too small and too slow to play in college! What makes this all the more remarkable is that NFL teams have spent millions of dollars developing a sophisticated system of scouting and talent assessment. They are the experts. If they don't see it, you don't have it. Right? Wrong. Bob, Daniel, and Wes did not allow themselves to be limited by the rash judgments of others. They encountered many people who couldn't *read* or see the truth but they chose to pursue their dreams undaunted by the swirling emotions and false assumptions that surrounded them.

* * * * *

If you think accurately judging physical and mental abilities can be a challenge then accurately judging someone's motivation, intent and culpability is like scaling Mt. Everest without oxygen, a rare accomplishment. This is why we are admonished with the words, "Why do you notice the splinter in your brother's eye, but do not perceive the wooden beam in your own eye?" and "Judge not lest ye be judged." The danger in judging someone without all of the facts is that we may be wrong. It's called guilty until proven innocent. On the flip side, it is likely that you have been falsely accused of doing something that you did not do. It is not only an unpleasant experience but you are forced to spend an inordinate amount of time and energy trying to prove your innocence. You might be thinking, "I would never falsely accuse anyone." But if you lack awareness of what is true, and the vigilance to continually seek it in your everyday life, you might be surprised to find out just how often you are doing it.

Whether you are the accused or the accuser, it is so easy to slip into gossip and character assassination especially with the proliferation of "reality" shows which entice us to enter the lives of others and judge them, often unmercifully. The eighth commandment enjoins us to not bear false witness against our neighbor. God is the source of all truth; his word is truth, his law is truth, and we're called to be witnesses to the truth and we have an obligation not only to speak the truth but also to seek it. The eighth commandment also calls us to discretion, in order to avoid the offenses of rash judgment, detraction and calumny. Although everyone has their share of faults and failings, there is no reason to spend an hour on the phone or in the coffeeshop talking about them.

There is a wonderful story about the sixteenth century Italian confessor St. Philip Neri who was known for his creative penances. One day a woman confessed to St. Philip Neri that she had been gossiping to others about one of her neighbors. St. Philip told her to go into town and buy a chicken. On her way home he asked her to pluck the chicken as she walked along the road and then bring it to him. She did as he requested and soon arrived with the plucked chicken. St. Philip said to her, "Now go back and pick up all the feathers." Aghast, she responded, "Oh, but Father that is impossible. The wind has scattered them in every direction and there is no way for me to get them all back." "Quite true," said St. Philip. "Just like the feathers, your words of gossip have been spread far and wide and there is no way for you to take them all back. In the future think carefully before you speak about any person."

However, on occasion you may be required to talk about the faults of others for appropriate reasons. But it can be a challenge to do it without defaming them or harming their reputations. Often in the course of my work, I am called upon to discuss the words and actions of many individuals. Looking for advice, I once asked a priest that I knew, "Father, when discussing issues about other people, is there some way I can be sure that I am not inappropriately speaking about them?" He gave me some good advice on the matter. He told me about the "three gates of the mouth." The first gate is to ask yourself, "Is it true?" The second, "Does it need to be said?" And the final gate is, "Will it make a difference?" If you can answer yes to all three of those questions then it is probably okay to talk about it. Taking the necessary time to be sure of all the facts, guarding your thoughts, and listening and thinking before you speak will help you to remain at peace and keep your emotions properly ordered.

In abstaining from rash judgments you will avoid responding with the inappropriate emotions, actions and words, all of which usually lead to poor performance. This is why the virtue of meekness is so important. It prevents the unsportsmanlike penalty that can cost you the game. Meekness? When you hear that word used to describe an athlete, somehow it just doesn't sound right, as if the individual is frail in some way or lacking backbone. So what is meekness and what does it really mean? It is the virtue of keeping anger under control. However, when we think of meekness, we sometimes tend to think of weakness. In reality, the two have nothing in common with each other. Meekness is the ability to be in control of our emotions. Therefore, a meek person is better able to use all their skills, talents, and abilities for the task at hand. Anger is a vice and the opposite of meekness. It is this inordinate anger that leads to the fifteen yard penalty, the red card, five minutes in the penalty box, and the technical foul.

Vulgar and profane language, which is often associated with a lack of meekness, has always existed and probably always will; but the big difference is that in the past it was considered unacceptable. Part of the problem today is that few people realize that there is a problem. John Wooden, one of the greatest collegiate basketball coaches of all time, is a great example and role model for anyone who appreciates sport played well and for the right reasons. He was a remarkable basketball player and coach and is one of only a small handful of people to get inducted into the Naismith Hall of Fame as both an athlete and a coach. He believed the essence of coaching was in being a teacher and mentor to his players. Coach Wooden saw sport as a tool for life; a means for developing virtue, and he exemplified that in the way he coached and mentored his athletes. Moreover, he was *both* a virtuous coach *and*, at the same time, one of the most successful coaches ever, proving that the two are not mutually exclusive. One of Coach Wooden's teams had a record seventy-four consecutive regular season victories on the way to an eighty-eight game winning streak. He had four undefeated seasons and he won seven consecutive NCAA championships—the most in NCAA history.

A lot of people seem to think that in high level sport, vulgar language should just be expected and accepted. However, John Wooden believed that trash talking was unacceptable and had no tolerance for it on his teams. In his book, *Coach Wooden: One on One,* he talks about how he never tolerated bad language. He said, "Sometimes when I overheard one of my players using profanity during practice, I would dismiss him for the day. My boys all knew that practice was where they earned their playing time, so I used the sessions themselves as a disciplinarian measure. If anyone cursed during a game, I would sit them on the bench for a while. It didn't take long for the players to clean up their language. There was no trash talk on my team." This story not only gives us some insight into Coach Wooden and his practical application of meekness but, more importantly, it clearly demonstrates that vice, specifically profanity, doesn't have to be part of the game in order to win.

As an athlete competing for the University of Maryland, I learned how to deal with inordinate anger in a most unusual way. I had just begun to jump high enough to compete on a national level and I was excited about the possibility of finally being able to jump in Madison Square Garden, the Spectrum, and other well known venues. The next meet on the circuit that I might have had a chance of competing in was the Philadelphia Track Classic held in the Spectrum. Usually only a very small number of jumpers, maybe eight to ten, from around the country received invitations to compete. Although I had jumped high enough to be included, I was unknown to them. My coach, however, was very well known and respected. He knew all of the meet directors well and he could probably get me into that meet. So I asked him if he could call the director of the Philadelphia Track Classic and ask if he would be willing to include me in the meet. Without any warning he started yelling at me and then stormed off! I was bewildered. Then, for a week or two afterwards, he wouldn't talk to me! Finally, one day, as he was walking by me, he said begrudgingly, "You're in the meet." I stood there in silence for a moment with a surprised look on my face and then managed to shout, "Thanks!" He still wasn't talking to me and this didn't make me feel too good but I tried not to dwell on it too much and moved on. Looking back on it now, he may have been just trying to keep me humble or teach me that there are no free lunches in life. Whatever the reason, I was in the meet!

The day finally arrived, it was my first really big indoor meet, and it required some patience since it was also the first time I ever jumped in the evening. Most high jump events take place in the morning or early afternoon. The meet was everything I had hoped for and more. The high jump had started about nine o'clock and by the time there were two jumpers remaining in the competition the rest of the meet had concluded. The amazing thing about it was that approximately 10,000 people stayed to watch as Dwight Stones, a two-time Olympic medalist and former world record holder, and I jumped off against each other in a great competition. I ended up in second place, but it was a great show, everybody loved it and I jumped well. The first person to congratulate me? My coach. He ran out from the stands and put his arm around my shoulder and he said, "Alright! We're going places this year." I immediately thought, "Okay, I get it. If you are criticized don't take it personally. Consider if it is deserved, if so, change, if not, recognize it as a problem of the one who criticized. The same holds true for praise: don't take it personally. If it is deserved, accept it with magnanimity and give credit to the source of all goodness, if it is not, gently educate the praiser as to why it is not due you." I learned that my beliefs had a lot to do with how I felt about things. If my coach was angry, I tended to believe there must have been something wrong with me. I let it bother me because I was too focused on me! I should have been looking outwards, trying to understand my coach and why he had been so harsh. I also learned that people, especially those who cared about me, were often reacting to the words I used and the way I acted rather than responding to me independent of them.

*   *   *   *   *

You will begin to gain control over your emotions when you clearly understand what you believe about yourself and others. Have you ever heard someone say, "Believe in yourself, if you believe you can do something, you will do it"? It sounds easy enough. "Yeah. If I think the ball's going to go in the basket then it will!" Well . . . not really. Your words, what you claim to believe, may initially make you feel better because as you've read, your beliefs determine your emotions. If you believe that the ball is going to go in the basket then you *feel* good. But what if it doesn't?

I've worked with athletes, notably tennis players, who had been instructed, "Act like you're a great player," almost as if they could build confidence without doing anything to deserve it. Picture yourself standing in back of the service line on a tennis court and a ball is coming towards you at over one-hundred and ten miles per hour. Either you have the ability to return that serve or you don't. You can stand there all day long telling yourself about what a great tennis player you are and how confident you feel—until the first serve is either ricocheting off your chest or rolling around on the ground behind you. As soon as that happens you have the proof, "I could barely see the ball, never mind return it!" You instantly have a new belief, "I can't return the serve." You are also no longer *feeling* confident. Isn't reality a wonderful teacher? Now imagine that you are able to return every serve and place it accurately in your opponent's court.

New belief: "I can put the ball anywhere I choose." Guess what you have now? Confidence. You don't have confidence because you *say* you have it, you have confidence because you can *do* it!

In stark contrast to the "tell yourself you're great and you will be" theory, there is the Dave Hemery practice of "doing what it takes to get the results you want." When I went to Boston University to do my graduate work and to coach, I was blessed to work with Dave, the head track and field coach, former world record holder, and three-time Olympic medalist, including the 400m hurdles gold in the 1968 Mexico Olympic Games. Other members of the staff included former world record holder and Olympic medalist in the high jump, John Thomas, as well as Joan Benoit who went on to break the women's marathon world record and win gold in the 1984 Olympic Games. Dave had a unique form of training which had helped him become the best in the world. I soon found out that a root canal would seem like a recreation in comparison. It is only with the passage of time, almost thirty years, that I can now thank him for *sharing* it with me!

Although I was one of the coaches, I was still training for the 1984 Olympic Games so I did a lot of my workouts with the team. On Saturday mornings, the track team would travel to Scituate, Massachusetts. In Scituate, there are sand dunes . . . big, big sand dunes. My first encounter with them is indelibly etched in my mind; we got out of the vans, stretched for five or ten minutes, and began the warm-up run through the narrow, soft, sand trails. We did about a mile in that thick sand at a pace that pressed the limits of my endurance. After all I was a high jumper! When we finally finished the warm-up, I thought, "Man, was that hard. I'm dead. I'm already exhausted and apparently we haven't even started the workout yet."

As I stepped off the trail into the clearing, I froze in my tracks. Towering above me was this incredible sand dune, four or five stories high and almost vertical! It made me regret that the warm-up run had ever come to an end. Dave very matter-of-factly told us that we would be doing two sets of eight reps on the big dune and that we would have to sprint each one as fast as possible. I looked at the mountainous heap of sand, took a deep breath, and thought, "Ohhh myyy goshhh." I remember attacking that dune for the first time. I was sprinting as fast as I could and I barely went anywhere; it felt like trying to run up a high speed treadmill, the belt moved but I didn't! With every step, the sand offered no resistance and just slid back down under my feet. Even though it was incredibly high and steep it didn't seem that far to run, but it still took me a good thirty seconds to get all the way up. By the time I reached the top I could barely stand, never mind walk. The lactic acid that built up in my legs deserved its name. It felt like the *acid* was burning through every muscle in my lower body. Coming down was in some ways harder than going up! My legs were so burned-out that I could not bend my knees to go down without collapsing. Because the down side was as steep as the up side, I figured a way to slide down by locking out a leg and letting gravity and my weight drop me down three or four feet with every step.

I managed to make it to the bottom, but I was immediately struck by the realization that I had fifteen more to go! There was something to be immediately grateful for, however: I was one of the few who did not throw-up. After running the sixteenth dune I thought, "Thank God! I made it! It's over!" This proved to be a false belief because shortly after finishing the final rep on the big dune, Dave informed us that we would warm-down on the small dune. It might have been lower, but it was twice as long! By the end of the session, I had used every ounce of energy in my body and I could barely make it back to the van. I hadn't understood why everyone who had run these dunes on previous occasions was so quiet on the ride down. I had written it off to the early morning start, but now I knew better. Saturday mornings would never be the same but I wouldn't have traded them for the world.

Dave knew the benefits that came with running these dunes firsthand. In preparation for the 1968 Olympics, he had run the Scituate dunes thousands of times and, if you weren't already impressed, he had run them with a tire tied to his waist! As he was waiting for his event, the 400m hurdles, everyone in the holding area was anxious and nervous, but all Dave could think about was the dunes. He knew that no one else he was competing against had gone through the pain and sacrifice he had gone through while running them. He drew lane six for the finals. Since each runner must remain in his lane for the entire race, a staggered start is necessary to ensure that everyone runs the same distance. This meant that Dave, in lane six, would be on the outside of the track almost thirty-five yards ahead of the runner in lane one. There would be no way for him to see how fast the other competitors were running in relation to himself. He wouldn't be able to see them until the final straightaway and if he was too far behind, it would be too late to do anything about it.

Dave told me that when the gun went off, he ran for his life, and all he could think about were all the dunes he had run. From the sound of the gun he exploded out of the blocks and ran like a man possessed. He kept expecting to see the other runners come up alongside him but as he headed into the home stretch they never appeared.

Dave won the race by the largest margin in Olympic history while setting a new world record in a time of 48.12 seconds. The photo finish tells the whole story. When I first saw it, I thought, "Where is Dave?" As I looked more carefully I realized that I had been looking to the left of the photo where all the other competitors were grouped together across the track. To the far right, looking like a man shot out of a cannon, was Dave Hemery crossing the finish line by a historic margin. He won because he had the talent and dedicated himself to developing it. His confidence came from knowing that he was well prepared and well able to run a time that could win Olympic gold. Unlike the tennis novice who sought to feel confident by *saying* words that were not based in reality, Dave was confident because in reality he could *do* what he said.

Take Away

Your beliefs determine your emotions. If what you believe is true, then your emotions, behaviors, and words will usually be appropriate. However, if what you believe to be true is in fact false, your emotions, behaviors and words will be the wrong ones and lead you to make rash judgments about yourself and others.

The next time you are confronted by a person who rubs you the wrong way ask yourself two questions. First, "Can this person *read?* Is he capable of responding appropriately in the given situation." Second, "Do I want to be in this person's shoes?" Are you attracted to his life and the way he lives it? If the answer to both questions is "No!" do what you can to help him; he needs it. And before you consider talking about him or any other person, ask yourself, "Is it true? Does it need to be said? And will it make a difference?" If the answer is "No" to any of those questions, keep it to yourself.

Recognizing the truth, the reality, about yourself and others is the basis for your beliefs. Your feelings and emotions are a product of what you *actually* believe, not what you *say* you believe. Do your feelings match reality? "Know thyself." If you don't like the way you feel, it's time to check to see if what you believe is true.

CHAPTER 4

Don't Just Stand There

M OST of us don't like change. We seem to like it even less if it means changing something about ourselves. We usually try to avoid it because it will cost us something: time, money, energy, comfort, or more. Even when you know it will be for your greater good you still cringe at it. Sometimes you're not sure whether you should charge ahead or turn back. Everything says, "Go!" but a part of your mind is saying, "Go back, this is a bad idea." Understanding the process of change while strengthening your will to overcome your resistance to it might help you minimize the pain and eliminate the procrastination that stops you from changing something even when you know it is for the best.

Almost everyone has jumped off a diving board at one time or another. Imagine that it is a beautiful, sunny, hot day and you're at the pool, and you've never jumped off a diving board. You're watching all these people jump and dive, and everyone seems to be having a great time. You finally bring yourself to say, "I'm gonna go do that, it looks like fun!" You walk over to the diving board. You climb up the ladder. You start to walk out on the board but as you do, you suddenly start to slow down. You come to the end of the diving board, and you stop. You look out. Two things are happening at that moment. Everything in you is saying, "Stop. Go back. This is a bad idea. You're gonna sink like a rock. It's going to hurt. Something bad is going to happen. Go back down that ladder!" Another part of your mind is saying, "No! I've seen people jump, this is fun! They're splashing, they're laughing, and I want to do this too!" Here you are at the pool, standing on the diving board. Everybody else is sitting around on their lounge chairs chatting and laughing, others are splashing and swimming in the water, and nobody knows at that moment that there's this battle going on inside your head.

For most of us, we eventually bring ourselves to jump off. Some force themselves to run off, screaming with fear and anxiety as they jump. Others try keeping one foot on the board as they attempt to slowly lower themselves into the water with the other, to minimize the height they have to drop. But eventually we all seem to find our way into the water. We go in, come back up, think "I'm alive! I made it!" and swim or, in some cases, doggy paddle to the side. We climb out of the pool and then find ourselves climbing up the diving board ladder a second time. Although you just went off the board less than a minute ago, the old feeling starts to come back: "This is a bad idea, don't do it." But this time, you don't hesitate as much because you realize that you were okay the last time. You ignore the growing feelings of fear or worry and you jump off again. By the fourteenth time around, the lifeguard is now telling you to stop running. You're doing cannonballs and splits in the air. You're jumping for distance. You're jumping for height! And now you can't even remember the first time you jumped or the feelings that had initially held you back.

That is how change happens. It begins in your mind, your wonderful mind. Typically your mind is of a greater power than whatever problem it confronts, but sometimes, especially in the case of psychological disorders, it is the mind that needs to help itself. This is a remarkable thought. It would be like a computer that has crashed trying to fix itself. It had the computing power to solve many complex problems but now the very power that used to solve those problems is diminished and, in its diminished state, it is not able to restore itself to full health. Fortunately, the mind is exponentially greater than any computer and therefore better able to recover from a *crash*. It is in the mind's ability to examine itself that you can overcome many issues both mild and severe. But how does your mind do it? What is going on in your mind that enables you to figure things out and take the proper action?

Let's go back to the diving board. Remember the first time jumping off the board, we struggled with fear, in this case an emotion based on the false belief that something bad was going to happen to us. This is often the reason we don't allow change to happen, the reason for our resistance. This is where *knowledge*, *reason* and *will* come into play. Knowledge is simply the mental process of being aware of something and comparing, identifying, discriminating, or connecting it to something else. Truth is an essential condition of knowledge. This is an important point because you can mistake error for truth and find yourself steadfastly defending a false statement when you lack one indispensable condition of knowledge: conformity of your thought with reality. Without truth you would only have the appearance of knowledge. That is why saying, "I think so" is a far cry from saying, "I know so."

Reason is how you make good use of what you know. It enables you to infer and arrive at a sound conclusion by seeing the connection between one premise and another that you already know to be true. Finally, with knowledge and reason, you are prepared to act. In a way, your will is reason put into action. The primary purpose of your will is to accomplish something good. Through repeated voluntary acts of your will, self-control is strengthened and good habits —known as virtue—are formed which on the whole build character. So if you can look at a situation like jumping off a diving board and say, "I know what it takes; this is reasonable. It's safe. I really *want* to do this," then just do it! If necessary, acknowledge in your mind that you may not like the feeling but that you're going to do it anyway. Once you've done it enough times, you will barely be able remember the bad feeling that came over you on the first jump.

Change often requires trying something new or something you never thought possible. What if someone told you to try and kick a basketball rim or the crossbar on a football goal post? You might be tempted to ask, "Is this person crazy or just not very funny?" There are some things in life that you are capable of doing but will never try because the thought never enters your mind, or even if it did, the thought might seem so ridiculous or outrageous that you wouldn't dare attempt it. Sometimes it takes another person who *knows* what you can do and who challenges you to see the reality of it. I had one of those experiences. One evening after an indoor high jump practice in the gym my coach looked around, then up, and said to me, "Thierfelder, let me see you jump up there and kick that rim." I looked at him confused and asked, "What do you mean?" He nonchalantly responded, "Just run up and take a pop-up and try to kick the rim." I said, "Are you serious? It is ten feet high!" "Yeah, I am serious" he said. I was a straddle high jumper. That means when I jumped, I would run in a straight line toward the bar, kick up my leg, rise up over the bar, roll around it face down, and land on my back on the high jump mat. I said, "Has anyone ever done it before?" He smiled and said, "Yes." Believing him, I thought, "What the heck. I have nothing to lose . . . except my dignity." I stepped off about ten strides, turned and faced the basket. A funny thing happened. I started to picture myself leaving the ground with my lead leg and foot above my head, rising up, and touching the rim with the tip of my shoe. All of a sudden it seemed possible. I ran up, kicked, sailed into the air and just like I had imagined it, my foot touched the rim. Ten feet! Afterwards I reflected on what had happened. I had a personal best jump of seven feet four inches, a thirty-six inch vertical jump, and as a long legged straddle high jumper, who was six feet eight inches tall, I could almost kick eight feet without leaving the ground! Instead of my incredulity about being asked to kick the rim, I should have said, "Of course!" Well, believe it or not, I got to a point where I could fairly easily kick a basketball rim or a football goalpost, also ten feet high. It really helped me with my high jumping because it trained me to jump straight up and it had the added benefit of making a seven foot bar look a lot lower! Kicking the rim also provided another bonus, at least for my coach. He would walk over to some unsuspecting soul and say, "You see that guy over there? I'll bet you a Coke he can kick the basketball rim." He would call over as if he didn't know me and say, "I just bet this guy that you can kick the rim. What'dya think?" In disbelief the poor soul would watch as I ran up, kicked the rim and landed on my feet. Another Coke, another proof.

Even if you are willing to enter the uncharted waters of "change," it doesn't mean it will be easy. As I entered my senior year of college, I was determined that I would become an All-American. I knew that I could jump high enough. The year before, I had competed in the U.S. Olympic Trials and the NCAA Division I National Championships. I reasoned that if I worked hard enough, I should be able do it. *Knowledge, reason*, and now all I needed was the *will* to pursue and realize my goal. In order to become an All-American I had to first qualify for the National Championships and then be one of the top six Americans to place at the meet. My training was going well and I had about ten meets on the indoor schedule in order to qualify. Before the first meet I made it known to everyone around me that I was going to be an All-American. This public declaration was not made lacking humility. I figured that if I told the world that I was going to do it then I would have no place to hide. I had put myself on the line not fully realizing what lay ahead. The first few meets went by without me qualifying for nationals. I got a little more determined and worked a little harder. A few more meets went by and I still had not qualified. I was now down to about three meets in which to do it. The next two: close, but no cigar. During this entire time I kept telling everyone I am going to be an All-American. Some of my teammates by now were looking at me with pity and saying, "Look Bill, we know how much you want to be an All-American but you haven't even qualified for the meet yet!" The last chance arrived. It was the IC4A Championships held at Princeton University. This was it, do or die. If *will* can become harder, mine became granite at that moment. I was clearing every height on my first attempt. The bar was finally raised to the qualifying height and only two of us were left in the competition. As I bore a hole through the bar with my eyes, I began the approach and before I knew it I had landed on the mat and was looking up at a crossbar that was still in place. My coach, teammates and I were ecstatic. I said, "See, I told you, I am going to be an All-American." They allowed me to bask in the warmth of that thought until we returned back to school. Out of charity, they sympathetically said, "Now Bill, it is great that you were able to qualify but you barely made it. At nationals, you will first have to get through the qualifying round. Secondly, even if you manage to do that, how are you going to finish in the top six!" Instead of weakening my resolve, the narrow escape at the IC4As only seemed to strengthen it.

As we departed for Detroit and the Joe Louis Arena, all I could think about was becoming an All-American. The opening height for the qualifying round was set at 6'10". Whoever cleared it automatically went to the finals, those who didn't went home. Everyone was given three attempts to clear that height, but one jump is all it would take for me to qualify. The next day I was in the finals! As the bar was raised to each new height, I kept close track of how many jumpers were left in the competition. Finally we had reached the height that would make me an All-American. First jump, a miss. Second jump, a miss. Third jump, a miss! But wait, as I was making my approach for the final jump a photographer walked across my approach and bumped into me as I was jumping. I was still lying on the mat with the fallen crossbar next to me in shock. I was thinking, "I didn't make it. I can't believe it, I didn't make it." What seemed to me like a lifetime was only seconds before the head official came over to me and said, "Don't worry it doesn't count. Go ahead and take your third attempt." I *willed* myself to shake off the traumatic event and refocus. If my *will* had been like granite at the IC4As, it had just turned to diamond. The jump was not pretty, I had planted my foot so hard I thought it would go through the floor. I was surprised that I ever got off the ground, but I did. And yes, I did make All-American but by the skin of my teeth. I finished seventh but there was one foreign national ahead of me and so I was the sixth American!

Sometimes, rather than dealing with adversity or our own issues head-on, we might be tempted to blame others for the difficult circumstances we find ourselves in. We lament, "If only this or that were different I would be able to get that done or do this thing." Performing at the highest level requires awareness of the facts as they really are and not as you might like them to be. It means being able to quickly adapt to any situation that may arise and take the right action. The next time you find yourself in one of these situations, think of this analogy. Imagine that you're inside a building and it's pouring rain outside. You go down to the lobby and you have a choice to make. You could stay inside, you could run to your car, find an umbrella, put a bag over your head, or just go out and dance in the rain. But I don't think you would sit out on the curb, getting drenched, and then yell up into the rain, "I *hate* this! I'm getting wet!" If you saw someone doing this, you'd probably think they were out of their mind. And yet we all do this at times. We sit out there getting poured on, and we complain about how much we hate it. Guess what? Get off the curb! Go do something else. Get an umbrella, dance around in the rain, or run to your car. Do something, but don't just sit there on the curb screaming about it. This may sound like obvious advice but sometimes, through a lack of awareness, we don't realize that we're just sitting there getting soaked. Next time it's *raining* in your life ask yourself, "Am I sitting on the curb getting wet, or am I getting up and doing something about it?" The only thing you can't control is the rain. It's raining. That's the fact, whether you like it or not. The question is: what are you going to do when it *rains*? By repeatedly exercising your *will* to act in response to the small difficulties of everyday life, you will be well prepared to handle the big ones when they come your way.

But what happens when you are faced with an endless stream of negative thoughts and no matter what you do they continue to wash over you in unrelenting waves? It's not the one drop of water that gets you soaked but rather the sudden downpour of a million droplets. In the same way, it is not the one-time thought that bothers you so much as the endless harangue. The answer is still the same: exercise your will.

Imagine one day the UPS man comes to your front door, knocks, and when you open it, he says, "Hi, I have a package for John Smith." Well, you're not John Smith. As a matter of fact, that's not even close to your name. So you tell him that. Then he shows you the package and asks, "Hmm, well this is the correct address, isn't it?" You respond, "That is the right address, but there is no one living here with that name." He says, "Well, that may be so but this is the right address. Please sign here, and he holds out the clipboard and a pen. You respond, "I'm sorry but I think you have the wrong house. There is no one here by that name." He is looking a little irritated and says, "C'mon, it's the correct address, I need to get going, please sign for it." The UPS guy will not give up, so you finally sign for the package just to get rid of him. You take the package and throw it into the living room. He comes back the next day, and you sign quickly to get rid of him. Then he comes back the next day, and the next, and the next, and so on. Soon, your living room is overflowing with packages that are not yours! Negative thoughts are like the packages. They are not yours, don't sign for them! It's not easy though, the UPS guy gave you a hard time and he wasn't about to leave any time soon. But, if you absolutely refuse to sign for the package no matter how many times you are asked, he will go away. The negative thoughts are not yours. Stop signing for them and they will go away.

You may be saying, "Well that sounds nice but how do I really do it? How do I say 'no' to the UPS guy?" There are many ways but they all begin with awareness. It may sound obvious but if you are not aware of the negative thoughts that are making you miserable and affecting your performance, then there is nothing you can do about them. If you are feeling unhappy about something, ask yourself, "Why am I unhappy?" Don't assume the obvious. What proof do you have for the negative thoughts and feelings that you are experiencing? If you discover that they actually have no basis in reality then use your *will* to stop them. The thought that is bothering you the most is usually not the first one that you had. It's actually thought number thirty-six. The first thought wasn't a good one but if you had stopped there all would be well. It's when you allow thought number one to lead you to thought number two which leads you to thought number three and so on until you finally are being crushed by thought number thirty-six.

The key is to stop that first thought before you begin to build
on it. One technique you can use is called "thought stopping."
As soon as you become aware of the negative thought that you
want to get rid of, yell "STOP!" Don't yell it out-loud or people
will think you're crazy, but in your mind, yell, "STOP!" Literally,
you've got to yell "STOP!" in your mind like you mean it, as if
somebody you love was crossing a busy street and was about to
get hit by a car. As soon as you yell "STOP!" refocus on whatever
you were doing before the thought came into your mind. Focus
on the details of whatever you're doing at the time even if it seems
trivial. If you are stretching, focus on stretching. Pay attention
to the feeling of each muscle as you stretch it. If the negative
thought comes back say, "STOP!" and refocus. Your commitment must be absolute. If the negative thought were to come
back one million times you would be willing to say, "STOP!" one
million and one times. You may be thinking, "I have so many of
them that all I will be doing is repeating STOP! STOP! STOP!
in my head forever." Try it. You'll soon discover that it will not
require "forever," only the resolve to go there if needed. Eventually you will notice that you are not saying, "STOP!" very often,
if at all. This is because you are no longer having the negative
thoughts. Your mind has said, "I get it. I'm not letting those negative thoughts in anymore."

Generally, it is the voluntary things that may be the most difficult for you to change, in part because you don't have to change
them. No one is going to "make" you do the thing. That is why
the hardest part about losing weight is not the physical exercise
but the mental exercise. It is the exercise of your *will* that determines if the pounds stay or go. You might say something like,
"I *know* I shouldn't eat this or that but . . ." "I know that carrying around too much weight isn't good for my heart but . . ."
If your *will* is flabby, you will be flabby. You will not exercise
and eat reasonably. It's January 1st and you pledge to make a

change stating, "I am going to lose twenty-five lbs. this year!" If you look below the surface, you will see that it was more of a *like* than a *will* to lose a few pounds. What you really meant was, "I would like to look good, or I would like people to think well of me, or I would like to be more athletic" but it really wasn't a commitment to anything. The comfort, satisfaction, and taste of food is far more pleasurable than the discomfort of moving and exercising. So why do it? Knowledge informs you that it is the right thing to do. Reason tells you that the relationship between your weight and health is real. Oh, but the poor old *will*. The problem is that you are waiting for the exercising of your *will* to feel like the pleasure that food gives you. Probably not going to happen, unless there is a strong enough reason. Can you clearly state your purpose, the basis for your decision? Is there something of substance to it? Is there a sufficiently compelling reason that will enable you to persevere to the end? If so, you will easily lose the weight.

About 15 years ago, I decided to give up chocolate and Coca-Cola for Lent. I loved chocolate. This was, of course, before I learned the real meaning of love. In reality, I just liked it a lot. Whole bags of chocolate doughnuts, Milky Way bars, chocolate milk—you name it and I ate it. Finally, I decided to give up chocolate and Coke. It seemed like my *will* flicked a switch in my mind. I didn't have the least desire for either of them, and I still don't. It's not that hard for me because I decided to make it my little personal sacrifice for God and I made an absolute total commitment to it. I never regret it and I don't feel like I'm missing out on anything. I share this with you to show why something like losing weight is really not that hard if your reason is powerful enough and your *will* is ready to act. You are in control, it is up to you. Losing weight—and a host of other challenges—is something that you can control. It's up to you.

But what about the situations that are thrust upon you?

The ones that you have not chosen and suddenly find yourself immersed in? These seem to be difficult and upsetting to deal with because you are not in control of the situation. Or are you? Your mind never stops working. You are always in control of how you will deal with the vagaries of life whether you have chosen to be in them or not. You may not like where you find yourself but it's like the rain. It's raining; what are you going to do? It may be of benefit and some comfort to know how others have dealt with extreme situations that they would never have chosen for themselves. Based on what they knew, using their reason, their *will* became the difference between life and death.

Admiral James Stockdale spent about seven years in a prison camp during the Vietnam War, euphemistically called the Hanoi Hilton. He and the other prisoners were frequently tortured and forced to live in the most brutal conditions imaginable. In an interview with Jim Collins, the Admiral said, "I never doubted not only that I would get out, but also that I would prevail in the end and turn the experience into the defining event of my life, which, in retrospect, I would not trade."

Collins went on to write in *Good to Great* about what he described as the Stockdale Paradox. He uncovered a surprising twist about those who survived the experience. He learned that the prisoners with the most positive attitudes frequently did not survive. Admiral Stockdale explained to him that the optimists believed the next big holiday would mark the date of their return to the United States and their families. They would be continually crushed by disappointment when the date came and went. They would say, "We're going to be home by Easter." But Easter came and went with no release. Then it would be by Thanksgiving and when it passed without relief, it would be by Christmas. With each setback the positive prisoners began to fall into despair and eventually succumbed to the inhuman conditions and, as Admiral Stockdale described it, they died of a broken heart.

Collins pointed out that the optimists failed to confront reality, the truth about their situation. They had hoped that the external situation they found themselves in would somehow get better and finally come to an end. When faced with the reality that they were not going home, they couldn't bear it. Collins notes that Admiral Stockdale and the prisoners who survived had a different outlook. They confronted the brutal facts about their life and chose to do what they could to make it better. They never gave up hope and *willed* themselves to persevere no matter what happened to them. Collins, who coined the term Stockdale Paradox, described it as the absolute unwavering faith that you will prevail in the end, regardless of the difficulties, and the discipline, *the will*, to confront the brutal facts, whatever they might be. This unwavering faith, acceptance of the harshest realities, and the decision to act, were the essential features of those who survived some of the most harrowing experiences ever.

Steven Callahan was an avid sailor, architect, and inventor. He set out from the Canary Islands, off the coast of West Africa, to sail over three thousand nautical miles across the Atlantic Ocean to the Bahamas. One night, about a week into his journey, he encountered some bad weather and his twenty-one foot sail boat was severely damaged, possibly by a whale. He barely had time to collect a few supplies and inflate the rubber raft before his boat went down. Knowing that no one was expecting to hear from him for several weeks he was on his own and alone.

The waves were so large that he was in constant danger of being capsized. After a few days his meager supplies were exhausted and he was left with a spear gun, a sleeping bag, two balloon-like devices called solar stills for condensing sea water into fresh water, navigational charts, a survival book, and a few flares. He was an experienced seaman and managed to do fairly well for the first week or so. But after three or four weeks he was really suffering. The solar stills, when they worked, provided very little drinkable water. The rubber raft was slowly deteriorating and required constant bailing and attention. He had to continually use the inadequate hand pump to try and keep it inflated and several times had to apply a patch in the middle of a storm. The spear gun had broken and he had to try and reach over the side and spear the fish that came along side by hand. He was developing sores from constant immersion in the salt water. Throughout the day large fish would slam into the bottom of the thin rubber floor, preventing him from resting and bruising his body. Sharks circled the raft. He barely slept. Remarkably, he never gave up. He resolved to do everything that he could to survive. He confronted the brutal facts but had faith that he would make it.

The conditions worsened! He was fighting to stay lucid. He was having trouble distinguishing dreams from reality. Despite the mental and physical torture, he *willed* himself on. He caught birds that landed on the raft with his bare hands and ate them raw. He was so desperate that he once grabbed the tail of a six foot shark as it swam along the side and pulled it into the fragile rubber raft. He stabbed it repeatedly trying to kill it without puncturing the raft. One thing after another, it just seemed to get worse and worse but he never gave up.

With the last shred of his *will* he kept repairing and innovating. He never surrendered to death although at times it seemed like the easiest thing to do. When he was lucid he acted upon his reason. With Herculean effort he did the next small thing, and then the next, and then the next. Despite the disappointment of ships passing by without noticing his little floating speck on the waves, he went on. Finally, after seventy-six days alone at sea he spotted land and was rescued by a small fishing boat.

Steven Callahan survived because he had confronted the brutal facts one at a time but never allowed despair to win out.

And there have been many others like him who have done the same kind of thing in even more desperate situations.

Poon Lim, a twenty-five year old Chinese second steward aboard a British merchant vessel which was torpedoed by a German U-boat during the second world war, survived the day-to-day torment and suffering for a record one-hundred and thirty-three days on a life raft. Three Mexican fisherman drifted over five thousand miles from Mexico to Australia, sometimes eating only twice in a month. They survived, by catching and eating what they could and by reading and praying from their bible, in an open boat for almost ten months! The stories go on and on but the common denominator is that they all accepted the harsh realities of their situations with an unwavering faith that they would persevere to the end. You are no different. You can do the same thing in your life when confronted with the most difficult circumstances. The only question is will you?

Most likely your chance will not come on the high seas. It is more likely to come in the small day to day challenges of everyday life. For many athletes, it may come in the simple execution of a routine practice session.

Let's say you go to practice one day and you just can't seem to get anything right; you're off, really off. You try to console yourself with, "Well, I should just pack it in today, maybe I need some rest or something. I'll come back in a couple of days and see if I can put it together then." This is exactly what happened one day while I was coaching one of my high jumpers. Greg was an outstanding athlete and had at the time a personal best jump of 7'3". One day he came out to practice and I set the crossbar at six feet for him to begin his warm-up. His first few jumps looked terrible, like he couldn't jump at all. He was hitting the bar hard, landing on top of it, and even after seven or eight more jumps there was little change. This was from someone who had jumped over seven feet! He was very frustrated and getting angrier by the minute and I could tell that he was ready to throw in the towel. My first thought was, "Maybe he's just tired today and needs a rest." I was on the verge of saying, "Let's call it a day and go again early next week," when it came to me to try something different. I asked him, "Are you willing to keep going?" Although his body language said no, he unenthusiastically managed to say, "Okay." I said, "Let's go back to basics and see if we can progress up to a full jump." I knew it sounded like baby steps for some novice jumper, but he agreed to do it. I told him to begin by taking approaches without a jump, working on being smooth and relaxed. After a few of those, I told him to work on the last three steps before lift-off. The approaches were looking good, his rhythm had returned.

Next, I told him to add a pop-up at the end of the approach, where he jumped straight up without trying to go over the bar. Soon they were looking sharp. Finally, he took his first jump and cleared the six foot bar by about six inches. He continued to work on bar clearance technique as I raised the bar after each successful attempt. Eventually I moved it up to 7'2", a height that he had never gotten over in practice and only one inch below his personal best, and he cleared it! This day that started out so terribly, with everyone ready to go home and wait for another day, ended up becoming the best day of his life!

Greg had felt like quitting, but he didn't. His *will* refused to give in to those feelings that said, "I'm off today. I need a rest. I can't be expected to be on all the time." He had reasoned that my judgment in assessing his ability was usually right. So despite his initial feelings of defeat he trusted what he knew to be true and acted accordingly. When you find yourself really off for whatever reason, try going back to the basics. Do step one several times until it is right, then add step two to step one. Then add step three. Eventually when you put the whole thing together, you are back in the groove, 1-2-3! Next time you're struggling with something at work or play, try it, you may be shocked to find that your best day ever was hiding there all along!

You have read that by the light of reason your *will* seeks the good. Until now I have only offered ways for you to see how it affects *you* personally. The good your *will* hopes to accomplish is more than your own good. Often the choices you make, and the resolutions to carry them out, significantly influence those around you.

Very often after a game, athletes line up to shake hands. I always assumed the reason had something to do with sportsmanship but if you watch closely you would be hard pressed to see it. From my earliest recollections, my dad always told me that when you shake hands with someone that you look the person in the eye, firmly shake his or her hand, and say something positive. He was right as usual and I have never forgotten it.

However, most athletes at the end of a competition walk down the line, the losers usually depressed and crestfallen, and the winners often happy for themselves and distractedly looking past their opponents for supporters in the stands. Sometimes it appears that members of both teams are walking down the line as quickly as possible to get the painful or inconvenient demonstration of sportsmanship over with as soon as possible.

Here is an opportunity to exercise your *will* and affect others in a positive way. Next time you line up to shake hands at the end of the game, look each player in the eye, firmly shake their hand, and say something like, "Good game," "well played," or "good job out there." Be sure to do it in a way that each of the players knows that you are acknowledging them individually by saying something directly to each one. In doing so you will be accomplishing two things: first, it's the right thing to do, and secondly, you may influence other players, competitors as well as teammates, to become better people by emulating you. It would be wonderful to see the post game ritual become what it was intended to be, a virtuous act.

Although relationships with teammates and those you love involve much more than a handshake, the same firm resolve of your *will* to do what is good, especially for them, is essential. Sometimes people think of relationships including marriage as a 50/50 effort like a business partnership, "You do your part and I'll do my part." That rarely works or endures. Imagine looking at two yard sticks lying on a table, each representing the commitment that you and your spouse have for each other. Often without realizing it, a marriage starts off with the two yards sticks lying end to end. It looks good, tip to tip. "See how close we are, inseparable!" you say. But in reality this is like the 50/50 model of "I'll do this and you will do that." As long as the tips are touching the relationship will work well. However, this will rarely be the case since neither of you is perfect and one or both of you will at times not be able to give your 100 percent to the other. In other words, the tip of one yard stick pulls away from the other and is no longer able to reach it. As soon as that happens the tips of the yard sticks are no longer touching and neither will the two of you. Instead of lying tip to tip, imagine the same two yards sticks lying side by side so that the entire thirty-six inches of one is next to the entire thirty-six inches of the other. This is the 100/100 model, where each spouse makes the commitment to give all to the other without counting the cost.

Let's say one or both of you is having a bad day or week, or month, or year! In the 50/50 model you will almost always be separated, never touching. In the 100/100 model the yard sticks may slide in opposite directions to one degree or another but they are always overlapping, always touching. In order to have a happy, good relationship with someone that will endure through all the trials and tribulations of life, you have to be willing to give

100 percent to your spouse, all that you have to give without reservation. This is not easy but with humility, gratitude, and especially sacrifice, which is love, you will gladly do it. The hardest part about committing to a good relationship is giving your 100 percent while not trying to get anything out of it for yourself. The reason most marriages fail is because they are entered into with the expectation and commitment of a business partnership in which each agrees to contribute some *part* of themselves. A successful marriage begins with the commitment to give *all* you have and expect nothing in return. No return on investment. If you love a person, you don't count the cost, you just love them and give them your 100 percent. You make the decision. Choose to give because you believe it is the right thing to do and not because you will get something back in return. If you are looking for a return on investment go to the stock market, not to those you love.

One of the challenges to any relationship is the fact that we live in a world that seems to be spinning out of control. It is estimated that in the past twenty-five years there has been more information generated then in the previous five thousand. The amount of information generated and the work expected from us is staggering.

It is estimated that the average person receives over sixty-three thousand words of new information every day, the equivalent of a two-hundred page book! During the past year over *five* exabytes of new information has been generated. You might ask, "What is an exabyte?" Well, to put it into perspective, one megabyte (MB) = 4 two-hundred page books; one gigabyte (GB) = 4,473 two-hundred page books; one terabyte (TB) = 4,581,298 two-hundred page books; one Petabyte (PB) = 4,691,249,611 two-hundred page books; and one exabyte (EB) = 4,803,839,602,528 two-hundred page books, and if stacked on top of each other they would reach almost thirty-eight million miles into space and could come to rest on Mars! In other words we are all very busy.

With my lovely wife, Mary, my ten beautiful children—Mary, Joseph, Elizabeth, John, James, Thomas, Luke, Ann, Peter and Matthew—and a job that demands more time than I have to give, I could easily spend the rest of my life anxiously running from appointment to appointment. But not only would it be the wrong way to live, it would make everyone around me feel the same way. It's important to approach life with the perspective of living in the present moment, "I'm in this moment right now, I'm not in that next moment yet."

So, I commit each morning to leave the house in a nonplussed and loving manner, never hinting that there are important meetings, appointments, or presentations to be made in a matter of moments. If I raced around the house looking preoccupied and loudly blurted out, "I only have ten minutes! I really have to run or I'm going to be late!" then everyone around me would have felt anxious and ignored. Instead, when I realize that I only have ten minutes to get out of the house, I come downstairs without telling anyone I only have ten minutes. I go to everybody, I kiss and hug them goodbye, ask what they are going to do today, and so forth. When they say something I stand still, look into their eyes, and listen like I had all day. I don't give any inkling that I am trying to get out the door. I let the little kids feel my beard, hug me with syrupy hands, I kiss my wife goodbye, and then I say, "Love you all, see you tonight when I get home, God willing," and I'm out the door. Mary usually walks me out to the car, sometimes with a few of the youngest attached, and we chat for a moment at the car window encouraging each other for the day ahead, and then I drive off with my arm out the window waving goodbye until they are out of sight. It took the same amount of time to be on my way as the frenzied approach but they don't have any sense of anxiety or feeling of being rushed, they got to love me, I got to love them, and it was a happy goodbye. I feel calm and at peace, and they do too. But I could have easily made the same situation upsetting for everyone by rushing around, "I've gotta run, I've gotta run, I'm late!" When faced with a "ten minute" morning in your life, what will you do? It's up to you, your *will*, to decide how to act in those few minutes. The health and success of your relationships, with those you live, work or play, hang in the balance. In both cases you get out the door and in both cases you get to your meeting on time but in one you are perturbed and anxious and in the other you are calm and collected and ready to face the day.

TAKE AWAY

Sometimes the game is not going your way. If it's not working, change it. Either change and possibly win or do nothing and lose. No matter how difficult the circumstance, if you have the knowledge of what is objectively true, use your reason to make good use of what you know, and exercise your will to put reason into action, you can make the changes necessary to adapt and survive in the harshest situations. It begins with the first small step and then the next and the next and so on until you are doing what you know is true and right. If negative thoughts creep in along the way that preoccupy and distract you, remember who's in charge and don't sign for them.

You always have a choice. No matter what happens to you in life, however much it appears to be out of your control, you are the one who decides how you're going to deal with it. Some people survived prisoner of war camps and others did not because of the way they thought about it. Just knowing you're in control of how you think makes all the difference in the world.

CHAPTER 5

THE PRESSURE'S ON

IS IT? Can you hand me "pressure?" No, because it doesn't exist! The thing you call "pressure" is all in your mind. It begins with the words that you use and soon after it appears to be reality when in fact it is like a vapor that can vanish in an instant. Words are your thoughts made visible. Their meaning can inspire heroism or terrorism. They reinforce your beliefs and ultimately express your emotions. Words are powerful.

How many times have you said, "I need to do that. I have to do that. I must do that"? You use these words all of the time often without realizing the subtle effect they can have on you and others. Sometimes you may use them as an excuse to explain why you are doing something you shouldn't be doing. However, when you believe that you have to do something, it tends to create anxiety and worry. Let's say that you and I have an absolute rule. Our rule is that you *have to* have a dollar in your pocket at all times. Now what if I told you that you only have ninety-five cents in your pocket. How do you feel? Most people wouldn't feel too good about that, because they haven't met the rule. They have come up short and it feels like failure.

Let's say that you work hard, and now you have a dollar in your pocket. As a matter of fact you've worked really hard and earned ten more cents; now you have a $1.05 in your pocket. If I asked how you felt now you might say, "I feel a lot better, now I feel good." No, you don't. You think you're going to feel better with the $1.05 because the rule stated that you had to have a dollar in your pocket at all times, and now you do. But wait, couldn't you lose ten cents? You might say, "You're right. Maybe I should have two dollars." Can't you lose a dollar and five cents? What you'll soon realize is that if you *have to* have a dollar in your pocket at all times, there is always going to be anxiety, even when you have the dollar in your pocket. It will never be enough because something could happen at any time like fraud, embezzlement, a recession, or a depression.

On the other hand, what if you just *want to* have a dollar in your pocket at all times? If you discovered that you only had ninety-five cents you would work to get the nickel because you *want* a dollar. If on the other hand, you have $1.00 in your pocket, you feel great. You have what you *wanted*. If you lose a nickel it's no big deal. Since you were the one who *wanted* a dollar, you would then happily work to earn five cents more so that you would have your dollar. It may sound like we're just playing with words here, but words are powerful. If you walk around believing that you *need to* do something, or that you *have to* have something, it creates anxiety and worry. I *have to* go to work. No you don't. What do you mean, "I don't *have to* go to work. How am I going to live?" Maybe differently than you do now but who said you have to live the way you're living? You will often say *have to, need to,* or *must* when it's something that is hard for you to do or requires a sacrifice. You say, "I *have to* go to work." Actually you *want to* go to work because it provides the resources to buy the goods and services that you like. By realizing that you *want* to do it, it changes your outlook and how you feel.

Imagine it's time to head home from work at the end of a long day and your immediate supervisor comes over to you and says, "I'm sorry about the late notice but I need you to stay late tonight to help with the new inventory system that we installed last week." Maybe you had other plans or you just wanted to get home, but now you are going to *have to* stay and work late. You think, "Why me?" It may be unfair but you need the job and you can't afford to get on the wrong side of your boss. Although you will stay and do the work, you are not happy about it. If another co-worker is also being "forced" to stay, the two of you tend to commiserate and complain about the unfairness of the whole situation. Your body language and facial expression alone would have been sufficient to communicate your displeasure.

Now imagine that instead of working for someone else you own a small business. You have built it from nothing with your own hands and it has required tremendous dedication and sacrifice by you and your family to get where you are today, but you wouldn't trade it for the world. You are not a millionaire, not even close, and the work is hard, but it is yours. You have a passion for your work and a great desire to serve others well. It is about five o'clock in the afternoon when you discover a problem with your inventory system. Your customers are expecting you to ship their orders tomorrow, so, without hesitation or emotion, you call home and tell your spouse about the problem and that you will be staying until it has been fixed. Your marriage is strong because of your faith and willingness to give all for the other. Your spouse completely understands and recognizes that when one of you makes a sacrifice so does the other. You are staying out of love for your spouse and family. Same work, same amount of time, but in the first instance you feel put upon and burdened while in the second there is no question that you *want to* stay. You are more than willing to stay and ensure the success of *your* business. Perspective is everything, in the first you say, "I *have to* stay late." In the second you say, "I *want to* stay late," maybe even twice as long if needed to fix the problem. "Want to" frees you up to perform well, be other-focused, and improve your relationship with everyone in your life. It is also a lesson to teach your children.

Joseph, our oldest son, who at the time was in fifth grade, really wanted to play on a local basketball team. Rather than organize the car pool and uproot the entire family, I said to him, "Well, there is no way that we can drive everyone around to a million events. If over the next year you can show me how much you *want to* play, I'll consider it." I never said, "You *have to* practice." After a year of practicing everyday on his own in the backyard he said to me, "Please Dad, I really *want to* play. I realize it will be a sacrifice for you, Mom and everyone else but I will do whatever it takes to play." Needless to say, he got to play. Every word you use and decision you make, one way or the other, has a consequence. They are your words, your thoughts, and your decisions. You don't *have* to, hopefully you *want* to.

I once worked with a woman who had called me because she was struggling to remain on the LPGA Tour. She was an extremely gifted athlete but she was having a great deal of difficulty performing well on tour. After working on a new mental approach to her game she began playing very well. In fact, she broke into the top echelon of players on the tour. One day out on the course, as we began one of our sessions together, she suddenly blurted out, "You know, next week is the really big one." I knew she was referring to the U.S. Open Championship but I didn't let on that I knew what she meant. I said, "The big one? What are you talking about?" With a look of shock and disbelief she said, "Are you kidding me? It's the U.S. Open!" I very calmly responded, "So what?" "So what!" she sputtered, "It is the U.S. Open! THE U.S. Open!" I then said, "I really don't understand. What is so big about the U.S. Open?" Now she was speechless. Before she could get another word out, I continued, "Wait a second, maybe I am missing something here. At the U.S. Open don't you still play on grass fields? Don't you get to use your own clubs? Don't you still use those small white things, I think they're called golf balls? Don't they have about eighteen holes that you roll your ball into?" She looked at me like the light was just beginning to go on in her mind and responded, "Yeahhhh." So I said, "Why is it the BIG ONE? Same game, on grass, with your clubs, a ball, and some holes." "Okay, okay, I get it," she said with a smile.

For all practical purposes there was little difference between the course she was playing on that day and the U.S. Open course at the Oakmont Country Club in Pittsburgh, and yet the words used to describe it, "big one," had the power to change her. The danger was in allowing her words to dictate how she would think and feel and ultimately play. If her goal had been to be as anxious, worried and distracted as possible then "big one" was the perfect phrase to use. If, on the other hand, if she only used the words that helped her focus on what she was doing, like "see the target," "feel my body," or "see the ball" without commentary, she would play at her best. The U.S. Open is really no different than a practice round except in one valuable way. It is a competition. But based on what you have just read, why should practice and competition be any different?

Timothy Gallwey offers a great analogy on the value of competition in his book *The Inner Game of Tennis*. Picture that you are a world class surfer riding along on a two foot wave. The wave is so small that all you can do is basically stand on your board and slowly glide along until the short lived wave dies out. It poses no challenge and you can scarcely use any of your ability. Imagine now that you are surfing with Garrett McNamara who recently broke the world record for riding the largest wave ever surfed off the coast of Portugal. *The Guinness Book of World Records* confirmed the wave was officially seventy-eight feet high! That kind of wave requires <u>all</u> of your ability. In fact, you will probably perform at a level beyond previous bests because the environment presents opportunities that just aren't there on a two foot wave. The large wave provides you with a unique opportunity requiring something that you might never have known existed within you.

At the U.S. Open maybe the grass is cut a little shorter, the greens rolled a little harder, or the pins placed nearer the edges. Same game, same you, but because it is a competition it may help draw out your best. If you use the words that help you to stay focused on the task at hand, and stop using words that distract you from your real goal, you will perform at your best. Avoid the words that create anxiety and worry in your life. Use words that help you focus on what you are doing, because the skills that got you to the "big one" are the same skills you want to have when you're playing in it! Using words like big, major, huge, important, will begin to change how you approach what you are doing and cause you to perform at a lower level because you are no longer focused on the skills, talents and abilities that got you there in the first place.

Part of the problem in sport today is that it is no longer viewed as an opportunity for developing virtue. In part, this is due to the fact that we don't use the language of virtue. When virtuous actions occur they are no longer pointed out and accurately described with the virtue they represent. For example, how often do you hear the word magnanimity used in sports circles? Probably never. You might not have ever heard of this word before because it isn't used very much. That is one of the problems in identifying virtues today: the words that describe them are not a regular part of our vocabulary. Magnanimity is an important virtue. *NewAdvent.org* defines it this way: "Magnanimity, which implies a reaching out of the soul to great things, is the virtue which regulates man with regard to honors. The magnanimous man aims at great works in every line of virtue, making it his purpose to do things worthy of great honor. Nor is magnanimity incompatible with true humility. 'Magnanimity', says St. Thomas, 'makes a man deem himself worthy of great honors in consideration of the Divine gifts he possesses; whilst humility makes him think little of himself in consideration of his own short-comings.'" Magnanimity is the virtue that allows you to accept praise from someone for something you did because you are keenly aware of and ever ready to give credit to the source of all your success, namely, God. The praise and honor you receive is His and in accepting the world's accolades you are accepting them for Him. This is not a false humility but a recognition that all good flows from God. It is your cooperation with His grace that makes possible the praise and honor. Humility is the recognition that, "I am nothing, I know nothing, and I have nothing." This is not low self-esteem but rather an acknowledgement of reality. After all, if you are standing next to God what are you bragging about? All that you have comes from Him and, as a steward, you are just trying to do your best to double the talents that He has bestowed upon you. The magnanimous man "never despises his neighbor, but esteems all men more than he does himself. If left to himself he prefers to be despised by men and to suffer for Christ, but if the glory of God and the good of his fellow men require it, the Christian saint is prepared to abandon his obscurity. He knows he can do all things in Him who strengthens him. With incredible energy, constancy, and utter forgetfulness of self, he works wonders without apparent means. If honors are bestowed on him, he knows how to accept them and refer them to God, if it be for His service. Otherwise, he despises them as he does riches and prefers to be poor and despised with Him who was meek and humble of heart." So the next time you win the prize, respond with a humble "Thank you" and offer it up to the one who made you.

Arsenal's slump extends to four straight losses in the English Premier League . . . Bill Hall is hitting .194 and trapped in a

1-for-20 slump . . . Jason Giambi was sinking in a 5-for-35 batting slump. What is this mysterious thing called a *slump*?

Dr. Jim Taylor has written, "Slumps are used to describe a wide variety of performance declines. As a result, there has been no clear definition of what a slump really is. For example, Webster's New Collegiate Dictionary (Merriam-Webster, 1974) defines a slump as 'a period of poor or losing play by a team or individual'" (Jim Taylor, "Slumpbusting: Overcoming Performance Slumps in Competitive Sports," *Sports Psychology Training Bulletin*, 1991). However, this definition lacks precision. Several factors must be considered in defining slumps. First, ability is important. That is, if the team was always lousy, their poor play would not be a slump. As such, current performance must always be compared to a previous level of play. Second, the length of the decline is relevant. For example, a baseball hitter who goes 0 for 4 may not be in a slump, but if he goes 0 for 25, he probably is. Third, a common aspect of a slump is that there seems to be no apparent explanation for the decline. If there were an obvious reason for the drop in performance, such as an injury, then it would not be a slump. Finally, a slump is subjective, i.e., a slump for one person may not be a slump for another. In defining a slump, these factors must be taken into consideration. As a result, a slump is presently defined as: "An unexplained drop in performance that extends longer than would be expected from normal ups and downs of competition (ibid.)."

Unexplained does not mean that there is not an explanation and reason for the drop in performance. The primary reason for a *slump* is a lack of physical and/or mental awareness during training or competition. Improving performance is relatively easy if you know in detail what you have done, your actual performance, and know in detail what you would like to do, your ideal performance. If you know the actual and the ideal, and you're willing to work at bridging the gap between the two, improvement is pretty much inevitable.

Then why are there so many *slumps*? Because most athletes, when learning to master their sport skills, never fully develop the mental and kinesthetic awareness needed to end the unexplained drops in performance. Instead they resort to using vague and negative words in an attempt to explain their sub-par performances. As a result, they are left hoping that the slump will end and their performance will magically return if they wear a new pair of "lucky" socks, or a "rally" cap, or try a new bat or . . . you get the point.

Let's say that you are a good hitter. One day, for whatever reason whether through fatigue or distraction, you strike out during your first time at bat. No big deal, everyone strikes out once in a while. The second at-bat it happens again. The third time at bat you begin to think, "I don't want to strike out again. I need a hit." But once again you strikeout. Not feeling like the game is going your way, you are fortunate enough to get a fourth at-bat and a chance to redeem a dismal performance, but once again you strikeout. You go home with head hung low and now you have to wait until the next game to make amends for your poor performance. Finally, it comes and you are fired-up and ready to play. As you approach the first at-bat the memory of the last game's four strikeouts comes to mind. You try to shake it off and probably would have if that first pitch wasn't a swinging strike one. Little thoughts begin to creep in asking, "What's wrong? I'm not feeling right." Strike three, you're out! The next two times at bat the same thing happens. You now are thinking, "This is bad. I am going to lose my starting spot if I don't start making contact with the ball." At this point you are still the same player that days before was a "good" hitter, strong, quick, and athletic. But something has changed. The words you are using to describe what is happening to you are faulty. They do not explain or describe why the strikeouts have happened. The words you are using only further distract and convince you that there is "something" wrong. The obvious problem is that you are not aware of what is actually causing you not to hit the ball and play up to your ability. If you don't figure it out, you will most likely strikeout again and sink further and further into the *slump* which, in reality, does not exist. You have fabricated this thing called a *slump* and you now feel helpless to do anything about it other than hope it goes away on its own. Sometimes it may appear that the *slump* did end on its own because, believe it or not, the words and thoughts that were distracting you and causing you to strikeout, may suddenly stop due to some unrelated extraneous thought or distraction. In that moment, if you happen to be at bat, your natural ability which never left you, returns just long enough to get a hit. Slump over! But there is always the fear in the back of your mind that it could return and if it does, you have no clue how to stop it.

The key is to stop using words that lead you to believe that you are the victim of some external, mysterious, cloud which has enveloped you and has indefinitely taken over your mind and body. Better awareness in choosing the words you use, and focus on the task-at-hand, will end a *slump* and steadily improve your performance.

Although the following example is about a professional golfer, I have seen it happen in just about every sport in which I have worked. The pro golfer, I'll call him Jim, was extremely talented and had scored many rounds in the low to mid sixties. The problem was finishing. During a tournament Jim would be on fire for the first two rounds, begin to fade in the third, and then completely fall apart in the fourth. Even when he scored well in the early rounds I noticed that he would begin to fade a little toward the end of each one. Because it would get progressively worse, and more noticeable round by round, Jim thought it was only occurring in the final round. This often happens in sports where you have a lot of time to think and "talk" inside your head. For many players who fade toward the end of a hole, round or tournament, the problem is suddenly becoming aware of the end. They focus on the consequences of not finishing well and think that this last shot or two really "counts." In contrast to many amateur golfers who struggle with their drivers off the tee, the *faders* are very relaxed and focused because they are not thinking about where the tee shot is leading, at least not yet. The second shot is much like the first, but as they begin to see or realize that the end is near, they change. They are suddenly very aware of every stroke and the finality of the approaching hole, and ultimate score. Thoughts and words swirl around inside their heads about pars, bogies, and looking good to whomever they are playing.

For Jim, there was no pressure teeing off. He was relaxed, focused, and usually drove it right down the middle of the fairway. Self-imposed pressure tended to build as he got closer and closer to the hole. He began thinking about what each shot would mean especially if it didn't go where he needed it to go. In a tournament, the same thing happened to him. The first day he felt pretty good. The end seemed so distant that he never gave it any thought. When he hit an errant shot in the first round he would say inside his head, "There are a hundred shots to go, plenty of time, no one mistake is going to do too much damage." That is how he would shake-off or rationalize the "bad" shot which temporarily helped him remain free and loose to focus on the next one. Toward the end of the round this became a little harder for him to do because he would become keenly aware of his score and his position in the tournament. The eighteenth hole was always a challenge because he would say aloud, "This is it!" By the start of the fourth round Jim would be almost exclusively talking about what he needed to do to in order to finish high and in the money. This led to not striking the ball as well as he could and adding strokes to his score. This intensified the internal rebukes of himself, the course and those around him. He would secretly say in his head, "Here I go again, the wheels are coming off." Not surprisingly, they did! For Jim, the last day meant the score was finally going to count and as he got closer and closer to the end the feeling grew ever stronger and every hole now somehow counted more. Jim would either think, "I'm on track for a great score! If I can just keep it going I'll finally make some money" or "Oh man, I lost three this round! I've got to make up ground for those three bogies on the front nine." But all of these thoughts and words prevented him from staying focused on the task at hand, being absorbed in the details, and doing everything that could help him to perform well. The score is merely a byproduct of performance, so using words that focus on the score rather than on the task, will almost guarantee a poor one.

The words you use to describe yourself and what you do can shape and influence your emotions and future performances. The labels you use to define yourself are often far worse than what anyone else might say about you. "I can't speak in public. I am terrible at this. I have never been able to do that. I can't . . . to save my life." Then the world piles on by adding more labels and creating the jargon that defines some new defect or disorder that will further define you. Could anything be more likely to assure the Yips than using the word Yips? You might ask, "What are the Yips?" The term "Yips" is believed to have been coined by World Golf Hall of Fame member, Tommy Armour, who said, "The Yips are that ghastly time when, with the first movement of the putter, the golfer blanks out, loses sight of the ball and hasn't the remotest idea of what to do with the putter or, occasionally, that he is holding a putter at all." He went on to say, "Once you've had 'em, you've got 'em." He said that the yips were the primary reason for his early retirement from the professional golf tour. And he was not alone. Many professional and amateur golfers suffer from this condition called the Yips. It is a condition that is most often caused by psychological thoughts and words that create a sense of pressure and stress so great that you literally can't move! Basically what happens—this is going to sound wild—you get up in front of the ball to putt, you line it up, and, you literally cannot move the putter. If you manage to budge it, you usually swing in jerky and erratic movements guaranteeing that the ball will go anywhere but near the hole. When it happens, it is very alarming and disconcerting because you want to hit the ball but your brain can't get your hands and arms to move in order to strike the ball. This phenomena also effects some golfers when they try to hit a ball with their driver. The club stops at the top of the swing and sometimes stays there with the golfer unable to follow through and strike the ball. And this doesn't just happen in golf, it occurs in many different sports. In baseball, there have been a number of catchers who couldn't throw the ball back to the pitcher. In dart throwing, the Yips manifests itself by preventing the thrower from throwing the dart, a condition that is sometimes called *dartitis* in the sport. Basketball players suffering from the Yips often can't make *crucial* free-throws or other *important* shots. There are two lines of thought as to the cause: one suggests that it is psychological and the other is that there is more of a neurological thing going on called focal dystonia.

"Focal" means that there is a specific area that the condition is focused and "dystonia" means the some muscles involuntarily contract due to misfiring of neurons in the brain. I have worked with golfers suffering from the Yips and, while it certainly could have a neurological component to it, I was able to help many of them improve and in some cases completely eradicate the problem. Therefore despite the possible neurological implications, there must be a psychological component at least for some individuals. Typically individuals who are very self-conscious and analytical tend to think too much about what they are doing and they can develop a fear of striking the ball. The fear is not of the ball but of the immediate judgment that will come when it is struck. To avoid the judgment they literally freeze up apparently unable to move. Ironically the fear of judgment they are trying to avoid is nothing compared to the embarrassment of not being able to swing their club. This tends to create a vicious downward spiral that often ends any enjoyment the game once offered and in the extreme, like Tommy Armour, an early retirement from the game. It is a difficult thing to overcome because the psychological thoughts that led to it happening become conditioned to physical cues tied to their swing. There are ways to overcome it if the individual is willing to work through it and let go of the words and thoughts that caused it in the first place.

For every athlete there comes a time when the days of training and competition come to an end. For some it is the only thing they have ever done well and it can be very difficult to let it go and move onto the next phase of their lives. This is why you often see very successful athletes, and some not so successful, hanging on far too long or continually trying to make a comeback. Their sole identity and self worth has been tied to what they did as athletes. When their athletic careers come to an end it literally feels like their lives are coming to an end. The main reason they feel this way is because they have never developed any other interest or skills and therefore have no idea what they want to do next.

One day I received a call from an NFL free agent who had played for a little over two years and he knew his career was coming to an end. He did not want to be one of those guys who desperately hung on bouncing from practice squad to practice squad or worse, playing in the Arena League until he was an old man. However, the thought of moving only seemed to increase his feelings of depression and anxiety about the future. He knew that I had worked with a number of players who had successfully transitioned to other careers and wanted to know how he could do the same thing. He had considered a couple of ideas that other players had tried but he really had no desire to pursue either of them. He had not saved a lot of money and he was worried that it would run out before he found another way to make a living.

He asked me, "How do I make a transition from sport to no sport when it has been such an important part of my life every day since high school? I love playing and it is the only thing that I am really good at doing." Listen to what he said, "I love playing . . ." No he doesn't. He means like or enjoy or find satisfying. But the word love attaches something to an inanimate object that shouldn't belong there. He finishes the sentence with ". . . it is the only thing that I am really good at doing." No it is not, but the power of those words left him feeling empty and afraid. Sure it is a difficult time with a lot of mixed feelings as some part of you says "go" and the other part says "stay," but that can't stop you from moving on to a better life. My dad always had great advice and he used to tell me, "No matter how successful and good your current position or career may be, it's good to have many irons in the fire."

That little bit of wisdom saved me from becoming a hanger-on. Two months before the Los Angeles Olympic Games something happened to me that changed the course of my life. I was so excited about the opportunity to compete in the Olympic Games. It would have been a dream come true if not for the jump at the 1984 Irish National Championships where my knee gave out and I collapsed to the ground. I instantly knew that was it, my last jump. I was not sad or depressed or upset. This may sound strange to you but I had been praying for a long time to accept God's will in all things so when this happened I trusted that it was perfect. Al Guy was International Secretary for Athletics and he was extraordinarily kind to me. Even after I told him that I would be withdrawing from the Games he strongly encouraged me to keep going and see how the knee felt in a few weeks. But I knew there was no way for me to be ready to jump. Fortunately, I had put my Dad's good advise into practice. While training for the Olympic Games, I was in the process of finishing my doctoral degree, pursuing licensing as a sports psychologist, beginning a small sports performance consulting practice, and best of all, meeting my future wife, Mary.

Dad believed that the more options you had the easier the transition and the better you will feel about making it. Of course he was right about that and I've always encouraged the players I have worked with to start developing other interests and skills early in their careers while they are still actively playing. This can be done in a reasonable way without distracting them from performing at their best during the season.

If you came to me one day and said, "I am not really sure what I want to do in life." I would suggest you sit down in a quiet place with a big yellow pad and write down every single thing you can possibly think of that might be of interest to you. Suspend all judgements about any one of them. Do not consider education, money, time or anything else at this point. Just list everything you can think of even if it seems wild or remote. Spend the time necessary to exhaust every possibility and then put the list aside for a little while. In a day or two come back to it and read through the entire list. Then read through it one more time and pick out your top ten choices. After you've done that, go onto the internet and actually research those ten career choices or things you want to pursue and find out everything you can about them: what kind of education and training do you need?, what are the salary ranges?, what are the time commitments?, what does it look like to work in those fields?, and more. Interestingly, after you've completed that exercise, I guarantee you, you'll probably drop out at least five of them. With the five that remain, I suggest that you go out and meet a specialist in each of those five fields. If you picked teaching in secondary education, go talk to a good high school teacher; if you're interested in orthopedics and sports medicine, talk to a orthopedic surgeon with a great reputation. Don't be concerned that you will be bothering them. They usually are passionate about what they are doing and they would welcome the chance to tell you all about it. Ask them what it is really like, day in and day out, to do their work because every job has its mundane—"regular stuff"—side that is far from exciting. You will very quickly get a feel for life in their shoes and whether you would like to try them on. By the time you are through visiting the five, you will have whittled the choices down to one, or possibly two.

There is a great feeling of clarity and certainty that comes from this exercise. It prepares you to move forward with confidence and a growing passion for your chosen field. The pro athletes that have done this exercise were surprised how simple and easy it was to find another pursuit that they could be excited about. For those in transition it gave clarity and for those still actively playing it provided a comfort by knowing that they could be developing themselves beyond football. It is easy to be content with the money made from your sport, but whether or not you need the money, it is a known fact that all of us want to feel productive by contributing and sacrificing, so it is still important to do even for a pro with a lot of money. If you're ready for a career change, give it some thought, try the yellow pad exercise, and don't be surprised if you end up in a much better place!

One athlete I worked with said, "I wish I had done better in school. I would like to have been a physical therapist in a sports medicine setting." I asked, "Why can't you be a physical therapist?" He looked at me as if to say, "Are you kidding? I was terrible in math and science, and I am twenty-five years old! It's too late for me now." This athlete was a very smart guy but he never applied himself to learning the prerequisites needed for a career in allied health while he was in high school and college. I said to him, "If you applied yourself to pursuing a career as a therapist in the same way that you did to become a professional athlete, I have no doubt that you could become a physical therapist. No matter how poorly you did in math and science, you could go back as far as necessary and learn all that is required for the degree and license." He looked at me with some doubt and I continued, "How long are you going to live?" "Eighty-five," he quickly stated. "Okay, eighty-five. Let's say that it takes you three years to take all the courses you should have taken in college. Then, say it takes you two more years to get through a masters program and five more to finish your doctorate. You would have your doctorate in physical therapy and you would be thirty-five years old. You said that you might live to eighty-five. You would have fifty years of being a physical therapist. You would be a physical therapist for longer than you would have been alive on the day you earned your degree!" You may use some of the same words "I can't," "I'm too old," "It's too late," and they limit you from becoming what you want to be, what you are capable of being. Often these limitations are self imposed and further reinforced by an arbitrary set of rules placed on you by society. The word "can't" means not able. Don't artificially limit yourself from doing something good that you *want* to and *can* do!

After one of my sports performance presentations a crowd of about thirty people, mostly coaches, physical therapists, and athletic trainers, approached me to ask some additional questions. They had surrounded me and I was doing my best to listen and to respond while maintaining some order. I heard someone start to ask me a question from almost behind me. As I turned to my left I was confronted by a Jewish Rabbi who was about

5'5", dressed in all black, wearing a long overcoat, hat, and a single ringlet of hair hanging down on each side of his temples. By the way, these ringlets of hair are called peyots and are worn to symbolize the separation between the front part of the brain, the more intellectual, and the rear part representing the physical, and conveys that the individual is keenly aware of the differences and proper use of each. You can imagine my surprise to see someone dressed like this amidst the colorful collage of Nike and Adidas workout sweats and shoes. He stepped forward and I shook his hand as he said, "I really enjoyed your talk and I just wish my son could have been here to hear it. I was never an athlete, and I am not athletic, so I can't show him anything about how to play baseball better." I looked him in the eye and smiled saying, "Come over here for a minute." Everyone who was still listening or waiting to ask a question stood back and formed a large circle of spectators around the two of us. During the presentation I had demonstrated how to use several balls at once to increase an athlete's focus and reaction time. So I said to the Rabbi, "You are going to go back and teach your son these ball drills." "But I can't catch," he said. I began slowly, and while I won't go into all of the details here, he gradually started catching one ball and within ten minutes he was catching two balls at high speed and looking like a professional athlete. The crowd went wild applauding his performance. His smile could not be contained as he beamed, "I thought I couldn't catch!" That one word "couldn't," which he used to describe his ability to catch, had held him back all of his life. That self-imposed word had come to limit him and prevent him from playing with his son. Are you sure you can't . . . ?

It is important to choose your words wisely. Even words that seem positive can subtly affect you in the wrong way. How often have you heard or said, "I am proud of you" or "That makes me proud?" You use the words pride and proud often intending to convey your feelings of joy for the accomplishments of yourself and others, but pride is a vice. It is an inordinate opinion of one's own dignity, importance, merit, or superiority that is believed to reflect credit upon oneself for something done or owned. Pride is focused on you and not the person you are attempting to praise. "You make me proud," is basically saying, "Something you just did somehow makes me feel the center of attention and deserving of all the credit." Why not say what you really mean? "You bring me great joy!" It is really joy for the accomplishment of another person that you are trying to express. It is amazing to see the difference in reactions when using the word pride versus joy. I use to say to athletes, "I am very proud of you," and they barely took notice or reacted to it. But now I say, "You bring me great joy!" You should see the look on their faces. They are taken aback for a moment and then they beam with happiness because it was their success or accomplishment which created joy for others.

I also find it interesting how we describe the good and bad things that happen to us in life. Have you ever noticed that when something really wonderful happens most people will say something like, "Boy, are you lucky!" But when the disaster strikes they are ever ready with, "Why did God do that?" Good is lucky? Bad is God? I don't think so. At least be fair and consistent, either all good and bad is luck or all of it is willed directly or allowed by God.

Have you ever watched one of those old 1950's newsreels about all of the inventions that would transform your life and make life a virtual vacation. The words they used to describe these remarkable advancements left the audience in awe and wonder. The viewer was told that once they had things like dishwashers, plastic bowls, blenders, microwave ovens, and other time saving miracles, they would have six to eight hours of additional free time each day! The narrator would seriously ask the stupefied viewer, "What are you going to do with all that free time?" His words seemed to imply that we would be desperate to fill our time since there would be practically nothing left to do.

Fast forward sixty years and you might be saying, "You've got to be kidding me! Now we're expected to do the work of ten people and there isn't a free minute left in the day." Technology and information has surpassed your brain's ability to take it all in. Like the viewers who believed the announcer, my Irish born grandfather, Popa King, believed that there was this thing called retirement. As he worked three jobs to make ends meet to feed, clothe and shelter my mother's family, he was told that at sixty-five he would be able to retire. This seemed too good to be true since he had come from a country where you worked until you dropped.

Like the technology of the 1950's newsreel, retirement was a new invention. The concept was to work very hard when you were young and then one day in the future you would be able to stop working and basically be on a perpetual vacation until you died. He believed those words. The words unfortunately misled him and set up a false expectation in his mind about what it meant to live a good and happy life. Keep in mind that retirement may have been set at age sixty-five but life expectancy at the time was only sixty-seven. Popa King lived to be ninety-six. That was thirty-one years after he retired! One third of his entire life!

Our grandparents were incredible people. They were disciplined, dedicated, and persevered under every circumstance and many made the final sacrifice in protecting our freedom and liberty. They knew how to love and sacrifice for someone other than themselves. They wanted their children and their children's children to have a better life than they had. The disservice to this great generation was in convincing them that at sixty-five life was basically over. No longer were they expected to sacrifice or work. Sure they would able to take some well deserved rest and maybe even travel to a few places that they had only read about but that didn't require, in Popa King's case, thirty-one years. Look around the shopping malls today and you will see many elderly people walking around trying to fill their day and maintain some precious contact with other people while trying to ward off the loneliness and feeling of uselessness they experience in each day of retirement.

There are, however, some people who didn't drink the Kool-Aid and in some ways may be more active helping others than when they were in their prime. I know many people in their seventies who are on multiple boards of charities, roll up their sleeves and work directly with the poor, and spend time loving and mentoring their grandchildren. Their lives are full. There really is no such thing as retirement, only a change in activity. As you get older you may back off in ways appropriate to your health and age but the good life is in the sacrifice and not the never ending time-off. Words, created in your mind or heard from outside, are powerful and can determine the kind of life you will lead. As a close friend of mine said, "At the end of my life, I want to be like a wet rag that has been rung out with not a drop left to give." How about you?

TAKE AWAY

The words that you use to describe your life reveal what you believe and feel about whatever you are doing. "I must," "I have to," "I should," create the false perception of "pressure" and they *make* you feel like a prisoner or victim of circumstance. It is important that your words reflect reality, what is actually, objectively, true. Use words that help you remain calm, focused and performing at your best. Phrases like, "I want," "I would like," "I will," "I can," "I do not want to do that," "I will not do that," "I cannot do that," free you up to do the right thing and to enjoy all that life has to offer you.

Even with the right words and a better understanding of ourselves and others, we can become frustrated when we fail to use all of our skills, talents, and abilities. We know they are there. We have seen them come out on occasion but they often fail to appear when we most want them to. Forget about how you measure up to the person next to you. It's time to start using all of your talents all of the time.

PART TWO

Making Peak Performance a Common Occurrence

CHAPTER 6

WALKING ON WATER

COULD there be any greater peak performance than walking on water? One of the all time greatest peak performances is recorded in the Gospel of St. Matthew when Christ came walking on the sea toward his disciples while they were fishing one night. But when they saw him, they were terrified, and said, "It is a ghost!" But Jesus responded calmly, "Take heart, it is I; have no fear." And Peter answered him, "Lord, if it is you, bid me come to you on the water." He said, "Come." Peter got out of the boat and began walking on the water toward Jesus. But the wind began to blow and Peter became afraid. He began to sink, and he yelled: "Lord, save me." Jesus reached out and caught him, and said, "O man of little faith, why did you doubt?" When they got back to the boat, the wind died down, and the disciples worshipped Jesus: "Truly you are the Son of God."

You might be thinking, "That is a miracle and not a peak performance. Peter had nothing to do with it." But consider what happened. Peter was not forced to leave the boat. He wanted to leave the boat and he wanted to go to Jesus. Christ made it possible but required all of Peter's attention and love. His free will was fully intact, and in order to walk to Jesus he had to act. When

Peter stepped out of the boat onto the water he was completely focused on Christ. In fact, he was so totally absorbed in the present moment and focused on Christ that he actually began walking on the water! If he had chosen to remain absorbed and focused on Christ he would have reached him.

However, something happened to prevent him from attaining his goal. At the instant he lost focus on Christ he began to focus on the wind and the waves and he became terrified. No longer focused on his goal, he began to sink! At least Peter had enough presence of mind that as he began to be swallowed up by the sea he called out to Christ who saved him. Certainly walking on water qualifies for miracle status but it required Peter's cooperation, his 100 percent attention, his peak performance. As you read the following examples you will find many similarities to this story. These extraordinary performances were possible but they required the full focus and attention of each individual. As with Peter, it was their cooperation with grace that resulted in a peak performance.

Alec Kornacki was working underneath the rear end of his thirty-five hundred pound BMW when it shifted and fell onto his chest. His twenty-two-year-old daughter Lauren was there and raced to the back of the car where she gripped the rear wheel-well, lifted it, and threw the back end of the vehicle off of her father. Her mother described hearing a primal scream from Lauren and an order to call 911. When Lauren pulled her father away from the vehicle he was not breathing and his heart had stopped. She immediately began CPR and was able to resuscitate her father before the ambulance arrived. He spent a long time in the hospital's ICU ward but he is alive!

Another remarkable story of superhuman performance at the exact moment it was needed involved a nine-year-old boy, Jeremy Schill, who lifted a car estimated to weigh 4,800 pounds, off of his father's chest. His dad, Rique, a farmer, had been working under the Ford LTD, which he had propped up on four jacks. As he was working the car shifted, and the front end of the car fell on his chest. "I started to panic because I couldn't breathe," he said. His nine-year-old son, weighing only sixty-five pounds, ran over to the front of the car and was able to lift the front end of the car just enough so that his dad could breathe. "Somehow he lifted it enough for me to get some air. I don't know how he did it," said his Dad.

You hear stories like this and think, "Well, isn't that extraordinary." But think about what this actually means. A nine year old, who never lifted a weight, never took steroids or human growth hormone, and who weighs a mere sixty-five pounds, was able to lift a 4,800 lb. car to save his Dad. You might say, "Well it was an emergency, he had adrenaline, something caused it to happen . . ." Of course, something caused it to happen. But regardless of the circumstances, it was a normal nine-year-old human body that lifted the car. The fact is that a human being can do this kind of incredible thing, but for some reason we have a hard time tapping into our full potential outside of extraordinary circumstances. And yet it's possible.

Peak performances can and *do* happen outside of extreme life and death situations. Consider Bob Beamon shattering the long jump world record by almost two feet in the 1968 Mexico Olympic Games. To put that in perspective, the long jump world record had only been broken thirteen times since 1901. The average increase of each record was two and a half inches. Bob Beamon broke the record by twenty-one and three quarter inches! Spanish cyclist, Miguel Indurain's resting heart rate of twenty eight beats per minute is one of the lowest ever recorded under normal conditions. Champion free-diver, Francisco "Pipin" Ferreras has the world record for diving without any external breathing apparatus. He has gone as deep as 561 ft. and is reported to have lowered his heart rate to 5 to 10 beats per minute while holding his breath for ten minutes. Research has been done on lamas and yogis who are capable of slowing their heart rate and respiration down to near imperceptible levels, in some cases taking less than three breaths per minute for extended periods of time.

Again, you may say, "But these are world-class athletes and holy men who live on mountain tops in Tibet, what does it have to do with me? Can a 'normal' person experience peak performances?" Absolutely yes! They are happening everyday all around you but often you are not paying attention to them.

One day I was in the garage cleaning out the car. My son Joseph was about four years-old at the time and he was exploring all the riches of a family garage as I vacuumed the floor of the car. At one point I looked up through the windshield to check on him and to make sure he hadn't discovered anything that would require a visit to the emergency room. I saw him staring at the peg board paneling on one of the walls of the garage. I don't know why I didn't go back to vacuuming but for some reason I watched him for a moment and thought, "That's odd, he is just standing there staring at the wall." As I watched him watch the wall, I noticed that he had a paint brush in his hand. Not one for painting the house but one of those fine art paint brushes. I puzzled over what he could possibly be doing. Suddenly, he raised the paintbrush above his shoulder and threw it at the wall. Spinning around and around in the air like a fan blade the tip went "thwump" and stuck straight in one of the holes! The holes in the pegboard were the exact diameter of the paintbrush. I just looked at it sticking straight out from the wall and exclaimed, "Joseph! How did you do that?" and he kind of shrugged and gave me an, "I don't know." I thought, "Well, maybe it's not that hard to do," and spent the next fifteen minutes trying to throw that paintbrush into one of those little holes in the wall. I even got up very close and rather than spinning it I tried to spear it into the hole. Not even close. But clearly it was possible. Joseph had actually done it. The challenge was in reproducing it. And this was not the only time something like that happened.

One night we were eating dinner and for desert the children were having popsicles. After they finished one of them dropped the popsicle stick onto the table. It bounced around and ended up standing on its side. Again, I thought, "Maybe that always happens." There I sat dropping a popsicle stick over a hundred times on the kitchen table and not once did it come close to standing up on its side. But it was possible!

Andy Panko is a basketball player that I worked with while he was in college and during his first couple of years in the pros. He is a wonderful person and an extraordinary athlete. Entering his senior year of high school Andy was a 6'0" point guard. He was a good point guard but apparently not good enough for coaches at the next level to recruit him. But, during his senior year he grew nine inches! He was now an incredibly athletic, skilled ball-handling, 6'9" point guard who could shoot the lights out. By the time he was on the college basketball radar screen, however, it appeared to be too late for the next season. Enter Division III Lebanon Valley College. They had heard about the local wonder and offered Andy an opportunity to play for the Flying Dutch-men. They were thinking they had found their star power forward or possibly center. Andy had a different idea. Rather than wait a year to see what might open up at the NCAA Division I level the following year, he approached the coach and said that he would sign with LVC if he could play one of the guard positions. The rest is history. He went on to set all kinds of records and was twice named Division III player of the year. He signed as an NBA free agent with the Los Angeles Lakers, and then with the Atlanta Hawks. Eventually he settled in Europe where he continues to enjoy a remarkably successful career that included selection as the 2012 Spanish League's MVP. What made much of this achievable, aside from suddenly growing nine inches and his incredible dedication, was the fact that Andy came to know that he was capable of performing at a level far beyond what he thought possible.

While preparing for a pro tryout after his senior season, one small incident occurred that convinced him of the truth that he had only begun to realize his full potential. Andy and I were walking toward the gym exit and we were discussing his shooting performance during the session. He was and is an outstanding three point shooter but I was making the case that he possessed the ability to shoot at an even higher level. He turned to me and stopped about twenty feet from the exit and said, "Coach,"—he called me coach even though I was not his coach—"you can't expect me to be perfect. I can't make every shot I take." I readily agreed but said, "You are far from perfect." He looked at me unconvinced, resisting the belief that he could do better.

Because I had been working with an NFL wide receiver prior to my session with Andy, I had an NFL football under my arm. I said, "It is all about mastering your ability to focus on a target. If you continue to improve that skill you could even throw this football through the hoop at the other end of the gym." He looked at me with a mocking expression and said, "Yeah right. If you're so great at teaching all of this focus stuff, let me see you do it." Without hesitating I looked at the basket, cranked back my arm and threw the ball with a perfect spiral across the entire gymnasium as he watched it swish through the net. Well, he nearly fell on the floor! He almost couldn't believe what had just happened as he yelled out, "No way, do that again!" I said, "Once is enough to make the point." I desperately tried to look nonchalant even though I was amazed that it had gone in! It was the perfect moment, a proof about what is possible, and planted a seed that has grown throughout his entire professional career.

Too often we witness a remarkable performance and write

it off as some anomaly or we watch in wonder all of the incredible pro highlights. Once when I was watching game film with an NFL wide receiver, there was a play where the quarterback appeared to have overthrown him. The player said, "That one was impossible; it was a bad throw." There were several things the he hadn't done prior to the catch that would have placed him in reach of it, so I challenged him, "You could have caught that ball." He argued that it was not possible, so I said to him, "Have you ever watched any highlight films?" and he responded, "Yeah, of course I have." I asked him, "What have you noticed about them?" "Well, they're great plays," he said. Right. In fact, they're more like extraordinary plays where athletes perform in ways you didn't think were possible and that's the reason you enjoy them so much. If you don't believe some feat is possible, it is not going to happen. If you say, "Oh, I can't do that," then you are absolutely right; it is almost a guarantee that your self-fulfilling prophecy will come true. Instead of viewing them as rare occurrences why don't you expect them all the time? After all, they were possible! And if they were possible, they are repeatable!

*   *   *   *   *

One of the keys to reproducing your peak performance is in seeing detail. The more task-related detail that you focus on during any performance, the more absorbed you will become in the moment. Literally try to see a scratch on the back of the rim, or the pin-point speck of dirt on your golf ball, or the lines between the grains on a football. You might say, "I can't see it." Try! Even in trying you will become more absorbed. That is what makes peak performances possible. That is what is meant by being in the "zone." The degree to which you improve your ability to focus on the details of the task at hand, is the degree to which you will ultimately improve the quality of your performances.

There are a few activities in which this ability to focus on the details is more important than in hitting a baseball. At the core of it, you are trying to hit a small round object traveling over ninety miles per hour with a round stick. Just making contact would seem a remarkable accomplishment, never mind actually trying to direct the ball to a certain location on a field or hitting it far enough that no one can reach it!

The *American Journal of Physics* published an article by Dr. Paul Kirkpatrick entitled "Batting the Ball." He wrote:

> Hitting a baseball has been described as the single most difficult feat in sports. And for good reason. Imagine the quality of hand-eye coordination required to make contact with a little white sphere traveling at over 95 miles per hour, using a 2 ¾ inch wide piece of wood being swung at over sixty miles per hour. Consider the intense concentration. A batter standing just 56 feet from the pitcher's hand has only about 45/100's of a second to decide if he'll swing, predict where the ball will be, instruct his muscles to move, and bring the bat to a point of impact. If all goes well, the bat and ball rendezvous a few inches in front of the plate. The ball is crushed to half its diameter, springs back, and is launched on its return flight at speeds close to a hundred miles per hour. Timing is essential. The difference between a hit over second base and a foul near first or third is a swing mistimed by 0.01 second. Baseball is the only sport where being a failure seven out of ten times is considered to be outstanding—only about a dozen players in each major league bat .300 annually. A basketball center who sank only 30 percent of his baskets or a quarterback who hit his receivers only 30 percent of the time would be selling insurance instead.

Given the challenge of just making contact with a ball, stories about players making promises to hit a home run in a major league game and then actually doing it, seems the stuff of urban legends. For young Matt Herndon fantasy became reality courtesy of Mike Sweeney, DH for the Kansas City Royals. Mike told me the story:

> We were in Minnesota playing the Twins and I arrived at the ballpark early, about three o'clock. Our PR guy came up to me and said, "There is this really sick kid in the hospital with a brain aneurysm, he is from Kansas City, and he is having surgery tomorrow morning." He told me that he had received an email at the stadium from Matt's father saying that I was his favorite player and that Matt's surgery was life threatening and asked if I would be so kind as to call his son today." Mike had a little boy of his own and quickly imagined all the anguish Matt and his family must have been going through less than a day before a surgery that might end Matt's short life. Mike's first response was, "Let's do it right now!" Mike continued, "I love to put a smile on someone's face so I called Matt, a little eleven year old saint, a sweet boy, and he just told me about his love for baseball, the Kansas City Royals, and that I was his favorite player. We just had a real sweet conversation. I told him, 'You be strong, I am claiming in the name of Jesus that you are going to get better. And when you are better, I'll bring you out to a ball game and you can be my special guest.' It thrilled him. I said, 'Are there any other players on the team that you like?' He told me that he really liked David DeJesus so I grabbed David and put him on the phone with Matt. David said, 'Matt, how are you doing?' 'Man, today is the greatest day of my life,'

said Matt. After they finished speaking, I got back on the phone with him and I said, 'Matt, I have never done this before but tonight I am going to try and hit you a home run buddy. I am praying for you and I am going to try and do this for you.'" Apparently, when Matt got off the phone with Mike he called all of his friends in Kansas City and told them, "Guys, I want you to watch the game tonight, Mike Sweeney is going to hit a home run for me!"

It was probably a good thing that Mike didn't know that this was going on behind the scene.

"Low and behold," Mike said, "the Holy Spirit blessed me and my first at-bat I sent one up fifteen rows in the Metrodome. I never ran so fast around the bases after hitting a homer." After the game Mike received a call from Matt, who exclaimed, "Mike you did it! You did it! All of my friends back in Kansas City started calling me, I didn't get the game on at the hospital, but my friends said that you did it for me!" Sometime later, a nurse brought in her laptop so that Matt and his family could watch the replay and share the special moment together.

For most of us the only way you know you had a peak performance is after it is over. Then we wait and hope that we can repeat it someday. What made Mike's homer so special is that it was a "called" peak performance. It was a proof that peak performances can be made to happen more often than you might have thought possible. It is not unreasonable to think that you can experience them too. In Mike's case, perhaps it was more than just mind and body coming together on demand. Maybe, because it was rooted in love, we see what can happen when sport meets grace.

*   *   *   *   *

The ability to hit a target at a great distance is one of the oldest and most recognized forms of perfection. A member of the United Kingdom's Calvary once found his mark twice by hitting his target over twenty-seven football fields away. That's over a mile! Now you might never have set foot on a shooting range before but there is a good chance that you have been on a driving range to work on your golfing skills. Some time ago I was working with a player on the LPGA Tour. Like most players she would spend hours out on the range hitting hundreds of balls. Even prior to the start of a tournament players would hit a slew of balls with the hope that this would somehow ready them for the competition. However, hitting golf balls for the sake of hitting golf balls, while attempting to burn off the mania that accompanies pre-tournament anxiety, does not make a lot of sense. The woman I was working with, I'll call her Carol, had weaned herself down to just hitting enough balls to feel the groove in her swing. She would only hit two or three balls with each club in her bag and that was it. She was ready to play.

On one occasion, Carol was beginning her warm up and pulled out her pitching wedge. The tournament's practice range was sponsored by FILA and their name was under each of the distance boards out on the range. Carol and I had worked together for a long time and so she was not surprised when I asked her, "What's your target?" She said, "The 'F' in FILA on the 100 yard sign." She took her first shot at it and her ball landed about ten feet to the right of the sign. Most of the women on tour would have been very happy with that shot but Carol had come to understand that she was capable of more. She also knew it was coming when I said, "Is that what you wanted?" Carol said, "No, I wanted the 'F' in FILA." I said, "Okay, do you think you can feel the difference between your last shot and the one that will hit the

'F'?" "Yeah," she responded confidently. On her next shot the ball sailed just over the 'A' in FILA. I looked at her again and before I could say anything, she said, "I know, that's not the shot I wanted, but I can feel the difference between the 'A' and the 'F'." Carol's next two shots went over the 'F' and on the third she actually hit it! You might be thinking, "Now that is an incredible peak performance. To hit a one foot letter from one hundred yards away is truly remarkable." And of course you would be right, but there is another insight to be gained here that might not be so obvious. The fact that she had the ability to actually hit the 'F' is certainly amazing in its own right, but perhaps more important is the fact that she might never have attempted it in the first place! In the past, she would have never even thought of doing it because she would've been satisfied with getting the ball to fall a few feet from the sign. Most players on tour would have been content with the near miss on the first shot. But Carol had come to realize that she was capable of more, much more. And so are you.

Another time, I was working with a golfer named Jim who was trying to earn his "Class-A" designation that would enable him to become a PGA Head Club Professional. The part he was most concerned about was the *playing abilities test* in which he had to complete thirty-six holes and score at least par plus fifteen. Jim was a pretty good golfer but he was very nervous about taking the test because he had a particular dread of playing in front of people. Not exactly the ideal for a club pro! I met him out on the course one day so that I could see what was actually happening rather than relying on his version of what he thought was happening. After about three holes I had a good feel for him as a player and I could see most of his issues involved his short game including his inability to finish well on the green.

On the fourth hole he had an approach shot of about one-hundred yards to the flag. In order to help him better *feel* what he was doing, I had him hit three balls onto the rather large green.

The closest ball had landed about thirty feet from the hole. As we walked up to the green I noticed that the grounds crew had just arrived and were ready to work on it once we had finished. There were two guys on mowers and four others helping out. As we stepped onto the green all of the workers leaned against the tractor to watch. This was Jim's worst nightmare, and it showed on his face. Jim stood in front of the first ball which was about forty feet from the hole looking like a man on death row.

In an attempt to diffuse the situation for him I said, just before he was about to make the putt, "I want you to close your eyes, hit the ball, and then before opening your eyes, I want you to tell me where it went, left or right, far or short." He looked at me with a confused but relieved look. He stood there for a moment and then, with his eyes closed, hit the ball. I watched as it went up and down, over and across, several large undulations and into the hole! Jim was amazed, the grounds crew was amazed, and I was amazed. I heard one of the workers whisper, "Didn't he have his eyes closed?" "Yeah!" said another. He walked up to the next ball about thirty-eight feet closed his eyes, and struck the ball. He sunk it! At that point the grounds crew was no longer able to contain themselves. Jim approached the third ball, about thirty feet from the hole, closed his eyes, hit it, and before he could say where it went, heard the sound of the ball hitting the bottom of the cup! The grounds crew went crazy and started applauding and cheering. Jim, who at the start of the hole looked like a wilted flower, was now ten feet tall and smiling. Three balls sunk from different locations, on a regulation green, from more than thirty feet away, with eyes closed! Incredible, but possible!

That's the funny thing about peak performances, they can show up when you least expect them. Not too long ago, I was invited by a national sports association to give a presentation on enhancing performance. At one point I asked for a volunteer to help me demonstrate a sports performance drill and a young man in the first row named Ryan quickly raised his hand, so I called him up on stage. I told him that he would have five tries with a golf ball and putter to hit an object that was placed about fifteen feet away. Then, as I did with Jim the golf pro, I planned to ask him to do it again, only the next time with his eyes closed. Remarkably, most volunteers hit more targets with their eyes closed than open.

I expected Ryan to hit one, or maybe two at the most, but he hit four out of five! I was crushed because the next part of the drill involves doing the same thing but with your eyes closed. I never had a time when someone didn't hit more with their eyes closed. But Ryan had hit four out of five with his eyes open. My mind raced to think about how to explain why the drill didn't work with Ryan, but why it was still a valuable exercise for improving performance. While my mind was busy formulating possible explanations, Ryan began putting with his eyes closed. 1 for 1, 2 for 2, 3 for 3, 4 for 4! "I'm saved," I thought. Then the unexpected, 5 for 5! Incredible! The place went wild, amazed at witnessing a peak performance that surpassed everyone's expectation, especially mine! I asked Ryan with some incredulity, "What sport do you play?" He said, "I am a wrestler." I shot back, "You're in the wrong sport!" Amateur and pro, young and old, peak performances are not only possible but they are happening all around you.

You might be surprised to know that a peak performance can also happen when you thought it impossible to create one. Once I was at a competition when I was suddenly hit by the flu. I became dizzy, nauseated, feverish, and fatigued. Despite feeling like a wet rag, I thought, "Well, I am here. I might as well do what I can." To my great surprise I ended up jumping a personal best! Although it may seem counterintuitive, sometimes illness or competing in poor conditions lessens the expectation and perceived pressure because no one expects you to do well.

This frees you up to actually focus on the task at hand which, despite the adverse conditions, enables you to perform at a high level, maybe even your best ever.

Another dramatic example of this phenomena occurred during the 1976 Olympic Games in Montreal where Japanese gymnast Shun Fujimoto did the impossible. The Soviet Union was easily favored to win the men's team gold medal in gymnastics. On his last tumbling run of the floor competition, Fujimoto felt a deep pain shoot through his right knee. He had broken his kneecap.

This is an extraordinarily painful injury because every time the thigh muscles contract, they pull on the broken bone. Rather than saying anything to his teammates or coaches about the injury, which he reasoned might distract them or cause them to despair, Shun persevered through the pain as best he could in an attempt to earn the points his team so desperately needed. His next event was the pommel horse and, somehow, he was able to complete the routine with a score of 9.5 out of 10. The landing, however, not only hurt, it did additional damage to his knee. Still, he tried to conceal the pain and prepare himself for the next event, the rings.

If dismounting from a pommel horse caused additional damage to his knee, dismounting from the rings promised a whole new world of pain and suffering. Just dropping from the nine foot high rings seemed inconceivable with a broken kneecap. Imagine the mental discipline and focus it required not to think ahead to the triple summersault dismount! Already in great pain, Shun was lifted up to the rings and began his routine. At this point those who had become aware of the injury held their breath. How could a man with a broken kneecap absorb ten times his body weight upon landing from that height? He flew through the air on his dismount, spinning at high speed. Then, not only did he land on both legs, but he nailed it! He scored a 9.7 out of 10 which was the highest score he had ever recorded on the rings!

However, he paid a price. On landing he also dislocated his kneecap and tore ligaments in his knee. The doctors who treated him after the event said, "It is inconceivable that anyone with this injury could have landed that dismount without collapsing into screams." Although Shun was forced to withdraw from the competition after successfully completing the rings, the Japanese team was so inspired by his courage and perseverance that they went on to defeat the heavily favored Soviets by the closest margin in Olympic history. Shun insisted that he be with his teammates for the gold medal ceremony and, true to form, he climbed the podium without assistance!

Another legendary peak performer who overcame injury and adversity to win Olympic gold was discus great Al Oerter. He was never the favorite to win. In fact, he never won the U.S. Olympic Trials! In 1956 at the age of twenty, no one thought much of his chances to place at the Melbourne Games but on his first throw he shocked the crowd when he broke the Olympic record and won the gold medal with a throw of 184'11"! Shortly after the Melbourne Games he almost died in a devastating car accident and many thought that he would never fully recover. Despite the odds stacked against him, Al found a way to win the 1960 Rome Olympic Games gold medal and break the record on his final throw of 194'2". Once again injury struck just prior to the 1964 Olympics in Tokyo when he tore a large part of cartilage from his rib cage. Doctors advised that the injury would require at least six weeks to heal and recommended that he not compete in the Games. With ribs taped, Al not only competed but won the gold medal and broke the Olympic record with a personal best throw of 200'1" on his fifth throw. The injury had been so severe and painful that he could not take his sixth and final throw. Al was forced to watch as the then world record holder

Babka took his final throw in an attempt to best him. Babka fell short and Al was the victor. Despite the injury, Al became the first man to ever throw the discus over 200'! By the time the 1968 Mexico Olympic Games rolled around, Al was considered too old to be competitive as many others had passed him by. To make matters worse, he had injured several vertebrae in his neck. While wearing a neck brace, he went on to win the 1968 Mexico Games gold medal and break the Olympic record with a throw of 212'6". Four consecutive Olympic games, four golds, four records, four peak performances, each a surprise. What are you capable of doing?

*　*　*　*　*

How often have you enjoyed watching all of the amazing high-lights from your favorite NFL players? I have personally wit-nessed many of these peak performances with athletes that I have worked with, but one that stands out in particular was made by Andre Collins who seven years earlier had been the starting weak-side linebacker for the Washington Redskins when they won Super Bowl XXVI. Interestingly the peak performance I am referring to occurred towards the end of his ten year career while playing for the Chicago Bears. At this point in his career, Andre did not get much playing time but he was dedicated to making the most of what he had left to give. He approached each down like it was the last one he would ever play. He made it a point to focus 100 percent of his abilities on the task at hand and to appreciate the joy and privilege of just playing one more play. As I watched him come onto the field at the Ravens' Stadium in Bal-timore for one of the few reps he would get in that game, I was touched by his great humility and in some strange way reminded of Hemingway's *The Old Man and the Sea*. There was something peaceful and deliberate about his presence on the field.

The ball was snapped and the quarterback dropped back to pass. As he released it, one of the defensive linemen jumped up and tipped the ball. It spun in a high arc toward the sideline about two or three yards behind the line of scrimmage. No one was within fifteen yards of the spot where it would land. Andre had been so focused and absorbed on the ball that he instantaneously began sprinting after it. It was clear that the ball was just too far away for Andre to come near it, but he sprinted like I had never seen him move before and did not let up despite the ball being well out of reach. He just kept coming, absorbed in seeing every detail on the ball, until his fingers wrapped around it about two inches off the turf. No one could believe their eyes. Andre somehow kept his balance, pulled the ball in while bent in half, and continued running at full speed. A second later he crossed the goal-line, touchdown!

Andre went on to tie a Bears' club record for linebackers that season with three interceptions, not including the two he made in pre-season, despite getting only about 25 percent of the playing time. He would often say to me, "I can only imagine what I would have played like at the beginning of my career if I knew then what I know now." This is from a Super Bowl Champion!

If you were on a team with Andre, you would be pretty excited to play with him. You would have a sense that with a peak performer like Andre, you could win any game. If you can imagine the impact of one teammate like him, now imagine an entire team of peak performers, including you! You might think, "That's not possible." Why not? If one can do it, why not two? Why not three, or four, or five, or an entire team? One time when I was speaking to members of a Division I football team, I said, "Picture right now, on your team, a player who is going to perform in today's game with all of his skills, talents, and abilities coming out right at the moment they were most desired. What kind of effect would that have on the game?"

Every player in the room agreed that, "We would probably win the game." Then I said, "What would happen if eleven players walked onto the field today and 100 percent of all their skills, talents, and abilities came out during the game? How would that team play?" They answered, "That team would be unbeatable!" As you begin to see and create peak performances in your own life, consider what life would be like if everyone in your family, at your work or on your team, joined in your commitment to using all of their skills, talents, and abilities in everything they did.

*   *   *   *   *

Since peak performances appear to happen regularly and are performed by individuals of all abilities, why don't they happen all the time? Or more importantly, why don't they happen when you would like them to? The first five chapters of this book go a long way in explaining why they are so rare. Certain things get in your way that can prevent your peak performances from happening.

Imagine that there are two, twenty-foot, parallel lines on the floor, about twelve inches apart. You are standing at one end of the lines, and at the other end a dollar bill lies on the floor. You're asked to walk across the floor, staying within the somewhat narrow lines, and pick up the dollar at the other end. You would probably look at me and ask, "What's the catch? It can't be this easy." I assure you that there are no tricks so you walk across, pick up the dollar and step off the end. You probably would have a puzzled look on your face that said, "What was that all about?"

First, how hard was that? Not hard at all. As a matter of fact it was ridiculously easy. Now imagine that the lines on the floor are a beam spanning across two skyscrapers, 110 floors up. Would you walk across that beam, given the same exact conditions, and pick up the dollar on the other side? No way. Maybe for a big pile of money you might consider it, but not for a dollar. Even then you would most likely wobble along with your arms out trying not to fall off or you might drop to your hands and knees and try crawling across. But why would you hesitate to walk across the beam when it was so ridiculously easy for you to do it the first time? One significant reason might be that you looked over the edge and saw the little cars and people down below. You think, "I could fall off and die!" But you had no problem walking across the lines on the floor the first time. In fact, it was so easy that you were thinking there must have been something more to it. It just seemed too easy. And it was! Without having to think about it, you were doing two things. You were looking at the beam and you were feeling your body move: left, right, left, right all the way across, saw the dollar, picked it up, and stepped off on the other side.

What happens on the skyscraper is that even though you have the same 100 percent to give, it's not being directed into seeing the beam and feeling your body as you move across it. You put nearly 100 percent of your focus on the little cars and people far below which leads to focusing on the feared and fatal consequence of falling off and being killed. Even if you attempt to walk across it, there's now a good chance that you *would* fall, because you're not focused on what it actually takes to walk across the beam (seeing the beam and feeling your body).

You may have experienced the frustration of not performing at your best. Somehow it felt like you didn't give all that you had to give. Can you ever be sure that you gave 100 percent to what you were doing? The most you can hope for when performing is that your whole 100 percent will come out when you want it to come out. The key is to know what it is that you want to focus on and then put your entire 100 percent of attention on those things.

Let's take basketball for example. You're on the foul line with only seconds left on the clock and your team is down by one point. The only thing that can help you right now to sink the shot is seeing the rim and feeling your body move through the right positions. If you put 100 percent of your focus and awareness on those two things, that's as good as it gets. But think about what often happens.

You go to the foul line, wanting and intending to give your 100 percent. In the background you can hear your coach yelling instructions about what you should do after the shot. Wait a second, what does that have to do with seeing the rim and feeling your body? Nothing, take away 10 percent for that thought. Then you think, "Mom and Dad are in the stands with the video camera." What does that have to do with seeing the rim and feeling your body? Nothing, take away 15 percent of your focus for that thought. The guy next to you starts trash-talking. What does that have to do with seeing the rim and feeling your body? Nothing, take away another 15 percent of your attention. You suddenly remember, "I missed my last two foul shots." Ouch, what does that have to do with seeing the rim and feeling your body? Nothing, take away 25 percent of your focus for that thought.

Add them up. Sixty-five percent of your focus is on other things that have nothing to do with seeing the rim and feeling your body. You are now standing on the foul line sincerely believing that you are putting 100 percent of your focus on the task at hand. In reality you are standing there with only 35 percent of your ability on the two things that will ensure you make the shot, seeing the rim and feeling your body. With only 35 percent of your focus on the things that can help you to shoot at your best, there is a good chance that you will miss the shot. That is why your peak performance doesn't come out when you want it to. Instead of focusing, in ever deepening detail, on the task at hand, you end up focusing on the consequence—good or bad—rather than the act itself. Thinking about the consequences of failure, or even of success, instead of the action often leads to the very outcome you hoped to avoid.

TAKE AWAY

Peak performances are possible. They happen every day. And you are capable of experiencing them more often than you think. Detail, detail, detail. The more you try to see, the more absorbed you become. It is the secret of performing "in the zone."

One hundred percent. That's it. You can't give 110 percent. There is no secret slice under the pie! Using 100 percent of your attention to focus on the task at hand, only on the things that are involved with what you are currently doing, guarantees that you will perform at your best in each present moment for the rest of your life. The good news is that there is more—much more—for you to learn that will dramatically improve all that you do.

CHAPTER 7

INSTANT REPLAY

WE'VE seen that peak performances tend to happen when you least expect them, and that often the only way you know that you had a peak performance is after it is gone. Imagine, however, if you were not only able to create a peak performance, but over time became proficient at reproducing them on demand. It's possible, but it requires that you become intentional in seeking them, have resolve and strength of purpose, possess an awareness of what you are doing, develop an intense focus on the task at hand, and remain in the present moment. That may sound like a tall order but you can do it! Although each little section in this chapter is far from all-inclusive, together they will start you off in the right direction toward creating and reproducing peak performances in your life.

> **FINISHED FILES ARE THE RE-
> SULT OF YEARS OF SCIENTIF-
> IC STUDY COMBINED WITH THE
> EXPERIENCE OF MANY YEARS**

Start by reading the sentence in the box above one time. Finished? I realize it may not make a lot of sense to you now but go back to it and this time count all the letter F's in the sentence.

Did you find at least three? Four? Five? How about six? Yes, there are six. If you didn't find six, go back now and see if you can see them. Still no? Then look for the three times *of* is repeated. Remarkable! They now look like an inverted *of* triangle jumping out at you!

Think of how much you expect from yourself and others with whom you play and work with each day. Consider the complexities of sport, including strategies, plays, rules, and so much more. But here you were only asked to find six letter F's in four lines and still you may not have been able to do it. Think of the times you have judged others or have been critical of a performance that required far more complexity. How was it possible that you did not see those F's?

Sometimes we can allow biases or preconceived notions to obscure our view and prevent us from seeing the truth. Instead of seeing reality, the details of the present moment, we see what we wanted to see or what we expected to see, rather than simply seeing what was actually there. Peak performance begins with being so absorbed in the present moment that we see every detail with perfect clarity. This requires the awareness to know that we want to focus, and then the ability to actually do it.

FOCUS AND ATTENTION DRILLS, TECHNIQUES, AND EXAMPLES

To give you some idea of what is meant by the word "focus," look at the picture of Babe Ruth speaking with one of the Belmont Abbey College students during one of his annual visits to the College. In the background to the right of Babe Ruth is a young man with light colored hair and a baseball cap set back on his head. Look closely at that young man's left ear and determine if there is any space between the bottom edge of his ear and Babe Ruth's right shoulder. Look carefully. *Really* look. Okay, were you just thinking about work? Dinner? Of course not. For whatever time you spent trying to see the edge of his ear, your entire mind, body, and spirit was in that tiny little space. You were completely absorbed. You didn't even know that you were in the room. Your entire being for a moment was in that small space. That is what is meant by the word focus.

One of the challenges to doing this often and for extended periods of time is that the activity you are trying to improve in eventually becomes commonplace. You no longer notice the details. If you play golf for example, you have probably seen thousands of golf balls. Over time, they have become little white fuzzy things. But really focus on seeing the detail on each and every ball, and your game will improve. With continued awareness and persistence, you will be amazed by how much better you are able to perform any task.

There is another tremendous benefit to seeing reality with clarity and precision. In addition to allowing 100 percent of your attention to be applied to the task at hand, it also enables you to prepare for future peak performances by accurately visualizing what you will do. When asked how he was able to make such accurate shots and perform so consistently, legendary golfer Jack Nicholas said:

> I never hit a shot, not even in practice, without having a very sharp, in-focus picture of it in my head. It's like a color movie. First I "see" the ball where I want it to finish, nice and white and sitting up high on the bright green grass. Then the scene quickly changes and I "see" the ball going there: its path, trajectory, and shape, even its behavior on landing. There is a sort of fadeout, and the next scene shows me making the kind of swing that will turn the previous images into reality.

Research has shown that peak performers visualize more than the average person. And this is no coincidence. Dr. Richard Suinn conducted a fascinating experiment with world class downhill skiers. He first measured the electrical activity in their legs by collecting EMG (electromyography) data while they were skiing. Later he had them sit down in a quiet room and visualize the downhill run while he measured the EMG activity in their legs. Remarkably they were the same! Despite the fact that they were not moving, the EMG activity spiked every time that they imagined themselves going around a gate. At the end of the EMG recording the researchers noticed a very large signal that they couldn't explain at first. They asked the skiers if anything had happened toward the end of their visualizing. The skiers said, "Yeah, we had to stop!"

I once worked with a 1500m runner who was having a great deal of difficulty hitting her split times during a race. A split is a smaller distance within a race, such as 200m or 400m, that is used to help keep a runner on pace so that they can run their best time for the overall distance. The woman, whom I will call Sue, was frustrated that she was not running up to her potential. During a race her split times were erratic and this would cause her to perform poorly. This was somewhat unusual because distance runners tend to be exceptional in their ability to feel how fast they are running, but Sue was not one of them.

I started by asking her to visualize a 200m run. This meant that she would be able to see and feel *every* step of the 200m. There are two views you can use when visualizing. One is watching yourself as if you were outside of your body watching from the stands. The other, which most people use, is seeing things from your own eyes as if you were looking out as you walked down the street. Seeing every step may not sound too hard, but give it a try. Imagine walking from where you are now to another room with your eyes closed. See *every* step without a break in the video. Could you do it? Probably not the first time. It takes some practice to see every movement without the momentary fadeouts between movements.

Sue practiced this for about four weeks. She finally told me that she could literally see every step of her 200m run. "Great!" I said, "Now do it with a stop watch. When you see yourself begin to run, start the watch and then stop it when you cross the finish line. Then before you open your eyes say the time that you just ran." At first she was all over the place. The actual elapsed time might have been 45 seconds and she would say 33 seconds. Amazingly over the next three to four weeks she became remarkably good at knowing the precise time she "ran" the race in her mind, even to the point where she was able to often hit the tenth of a second. The really exciting part was that her times on the track just kept getting better. She was hitting every split and was able to run the entire race on pace. Sue finished the season with a personal best in the 1500m and qualified for the National Championships.

A little exercise that may help your ability to see things more clearly entails looking at a photograph for thirty seconds and then putting it aside out of view and drawing what you saw. How it looks is not as important as whether you captured all of the details. At first you will probably be surprised how little you are able to capture. The trick is in not remembering some list of objects but simply seeing the photo in your mind's eye. If this proves too challenging try staring at the photo for a few seconds and then close your eyes for a few seconds, seeing the imprint in your mind, then open your eyes and stare at it again, repeating this for a minute or two. You will be amazed at how well you begin to see things with your eyes closed and opened!

This ability to see and focus in detail does far more than just help you master technique or improve your timing; it is a game changer. Consider that an NFL quarterback has less than four seconds to find and deliver a ball to an open receiver before being sacked. You might say, "Well, that's not so fast." Could you find someone in a crowded room in four seconds? Maybe. But could you locate another three people in different parts of the room before finding the one you wanted to speak with? That's what a NFL QB does on almost every play. Even before the ball is snapped he is looking at the field and watching the movement of the defense. He typically has four or five options toward whom to throw when the ball is snapped. Amazingly as he looks through his progression, he sees instantly if the first receiver is open before he is even a quarter of the way through the pattern. It is like watching a video and pressing pause at the one second mark. What do you see? Based on that limited view will the receiver be open. It is either throw or not throw. If not, press play for one more second. What do you see? Throw or not throw? If the next receiver in the progression will not be open, press play again for one second. This continues for about four seconds until the QB is either sacked or has thrown the pass.

On the other side of the ball, the linebacker or defensive back must cover the receiver. If he only sees a blur of the player in front of him, he will be faked-out and beaten. His ability to focus on a detailed spot on the player he is covering is essential if he hopes to stay close enough to prevent a completion. His ability to then shift his laser-like focus to the ball is what makes an interception possible. The better he is at doing that the more likely it is that he will achieve peak performance.

This is not only true for football; almost every sport requires that same kind of ability to see things in great detail. Think of the intense visual focus needed to return a 120 mph serve in tennis. It takes about 100 milliseconds to process visual cues and locate a ball in space. Once you see the ball it will take another 75 milliseconds for your brain to calculate the speed, spin, and direction of the ball. Fifty more milliseconds to choose the direction that you will move. Twenty-five milliseconds to trigger your muscles to fire and begin moving in that direction. At this point the ball is at the net. You now have less than four-tenths of a second to cover the distance in order to make contact with the ball. The difference between amateur and professional players is their ability to see subtle cues that indicate where the serve will go. With so little time to respond their ability to see what is happening with perfect clarity is essential. The pros see cues that tell them where the ball is going before it is hit. They see the smallest changes in the hip, shoulder, and racquet movements of the server, whereas the amateur only sees the ball after it comes off the racquet.

Consider a simple task like standing twenty feet away from someone who is holding a hula-hoop three or four feet above the ground like a basket. You are given three golf balls and asked to toss them one at a time through the hoop. You might be fairly confident that you will throw all three of them through it, but sometimes you can get that funny feeling, especially when something seems really easy to do, where you think, "I hope they all go in." You could even have a close call on one of them or it might be possible that you actually hit the rim or miss one completely. With just a small change in focus and perception the result could be very different. If instead of tossing the golf ball through a hula-hoop, you were asked to toss it into an egg cup suspended in the middle of the hula-hoop, what do you think the result would be? You might be thinking, "That would be a lot harder to do." Surely it would be more challenging but is there any doubt in your mind that all of the balls would easily go through the hula-hoop?

Seeing clearly what is happening in the here-and-now is essential to peak performance. But life is made up of a lot of here-and-nows. If you live eighty years, you will have 2,522,880,000 seconds of life, or 2.5 billion present moments. If you are forty years old, you only have about 1.25 billion remaining. That may seem like a lot of time but think of how quickly the first half has flown by! Moving from present moment to present moment is not only part of life but it is an essential element of reproducing peak performances. If in this present moment you are visualizing, then focus on visualizing. If you do it for five minutes, then that is 300 present moments spent focused on visualizing. If in the next present moment you are swinging a club, then focus on feeling your swing. If in another present moment you are reflecting on what actually happened, then focus on recalling and feeling what you did. In yet another present moment you could be planning what to do to improve your training, then focus on planning. The key is to focus exclusively on the intent of each particular present moment. Adding anything else is a waste of your time and talent.

MASTERING TECHNIQUE: KINESTHETIC AWARENESS AND MOTOR LEARNING & CONTROL

Performing at your best in the present moment is also affected by your ability to feel the sensation of movement. This is sometimes referred to as kinesthetic awareness or your ability to know where your body is in space. At this moment you are holding this book, or possibly an electronic reader. Freeze! Don't move. Don't look. Where is your right middle finger? You might tell me, "It is touching the back of the book." Okay, where is the pressure on that finger? Is it toward the left, right, or middle of your finger? You say, "It is on the left side of my middle finger." Is it more toward the tip, middle, or lower part of your finger? "The middle," you say. How were you able to know it? Because you could feel it! This may seem simplistic, but it is the essence of mastering movement and technique in any sport, fine art or craft.

Here's a simple drill to improve your kinesthetic awareness. Put a pen on the table in front of you, maybe about 18 or 20 inches away with the point facing towards you. Then bring your hands back to the edge of the table and stare at the tip of the pen. After you've stared at it for a few seconds, close your eyes, and with your right index finger reach out and touch the tip of the pen. Now, when you reach out, don't feel around for the pen, just put your finger down firmly wherever you think the pen tip is located. Don't open your eyes yet! If you did not touch it, ask yourself, "Where am I? Is my finger short or long, right or left, in relation to the tip of the pen?" Then open your eyes and look at where your finger is on the table compared to where you said it was on the table. Resist the self-critical negative commentary, and just observe the difference. At first you might not be able to know where your finger landed on the table, but after five or six tries, you'll find that your sense of movement and position begins to improve.

If you find that you are having difficulty feeling where you are on the table after several tries, pause when you open your eyes and feel where your finger is on the table. Feel the angles of your arm, elbow and shoulder. Then move your finger to the pen tip and feel the difference. Go back and forth several times, pausing at each point to really feel the difference between them. It won't take many more tries to touch the pen tip with your eyes closed. You will probably smile when you finally touch the pen tip but what was the goal of this drill? Many athletes will say, "To touch the pen tip." No. The goal was to know where your finger was on the table! Think of it this way, if you know where your finger is every time, can't you eventually put it where you want it to go? By improving this ability to know where your body is in space, you will dramatically improve the way you perform at almost anything that you do.

Often a coach will immediately tell a player what he or she did "wrong" and then what they should do the next time. This approach, however, slows down the learning process and almost ensures future errors. The reason the error occurred in the first place is because the athlete doesn't know what happened. How can an athlete improve some aspect of his technique when he doesn't know what he did in the first place? Often coaches and athletes will guess at what happened rather than knowing what happened. They become like Sherlock Homes and try to use their deductive reasoning. "Well, if the ball went . . . , I must have done . . ." They don't know the answer and therefore they don't have a clue about how to change from what they did to what they wanted to do.

While giving a presentation to the United States Intercollegiate Lacrosse Association, I asked the coaches in attendance, "How many basketballs can fit, side by side, through a basketball hoop?" Quickly one of the coaches shot back with the correct answer, "Two!" I then asked them, "How many lacrosse balls can fit, side by side, through a lacrosse goal?" The room went silent, filled with blank stares. This was the U.S. Intercollegiate Lacrosse Association, shouldn't they know that? The answer is 784! They all looked at me skeptically. But it's true. The goal opening is six feet by six feet or seventy-two inches by seventy-two inches. Each lacrosse ball is two and a half inches across. That means twenty-eight balls fit across the width of the goal and 28 balls fit from top to bottom. Twenty-eight times twenty-eight = 784! Even with a monster sized goalie in front of the goal, he would only block out 434 balls. That means there are still 350 potential scoring opportunities!

The coaches were just beginning to comprehend the full magnitude of this fact and how much it would help their players perfect the skill required to shoot a ball through any one of those openings. I told them to imagine 784 balls across the front of a lacrosse goal numbered 1 through 784 four. Then I asked them to imagine one of their players being able to hit any one of them, such as number 56, on command. Let's say he takes the shot but instead of hitting number 56 he hits number 60. You might think, "That's not too bad." However, consider that missing the target by four balls means that he was off by ten inches. Ten inches can easily be the difference between a shot bouncing off the goal frame or being blocked by the goalie's stick. Developing the skill to hit number 56 begins with knowing that the target is precisely number 56 and not number 57 or 55.

There is a world of difference between this precision targeting and shooting toward a general space like the upper or lower corner of the goal. With the intent and focus to hit a specific two and a half inch hole, an athlete will quickly improve his or her ability to feel the difference between any number on the goal. This ability to feel the subtlest changes in force and direction is the key to accuracy and consistency. If you worked on this kind of awareness in whatever activity you are doing, you would become like a human highlight film.

You might say, "That sounds great but how do you actually do it? How do you learn to feel the subtle difference between the movements that result in hitting number 56 and not 55 or 57?" Good question. Let's say a basketball player has been inconsistent with his free throw shooting. The problem is that his elbow keeps flying out to the side each time he shoots the ball. Most coaches would tell him, "Okay look, you've got to keep your elbow in line with the shot" and the player would say something like, "Gotcha coach." He takes another shot and, again, the elbow flies out to the side. The coach says, "Now what did I tell you?" "Keep your elbow in line with the shot," the player responds. Coach says, "Right! Now keep the elbow in." He takes a few more shots, and each time the same thing happens: his elbow flies out to the side. The same thing keeps happening, again, and again, and again. The coach gets a little annoyed or frustrated at this point, but it's not as if the player is purposefully throwing his elbow out to the side. But it keeps happening.

There needs to be a different approach. So let's think about this logically. If his elbow keeps going out to the side even though he wants to keep it in line with the ball, it means that he can't feel what his elbow is doing when he is shooting. Here's what the coach could do to help him. Have the player stand on the foul line in his shooting stance with the ball over his head as it would be during a free throw. Next, raise his shooting elbow as far away from his body as possible while he holds the shooting position and tell him, "That elbow position is a one." Lower his elbow two or three more inches and tell him, "That is a two." Move it down a few more inches and call that a three, two more inches lower would be a four, and, finally, you would move the elbow directly in line with the ball and say, "That's a five."

The coach moves him through all five positions several times, stopping at each one, to emphasize the feeling of his elbow and shoulder with each number. Coach never says, "Try to get a five." His goal is not to get a five. His goal is to feel how his elbow and shoulder move during the shot. Then, the coach says, "Take a shot and give me a number." After he takes his shot you say, "Give me a number." The first time he's asked, the player might shoot, and then hesitantly respond, "Uhh, a three?" The question mark says, "I don't really know or I am not sure." While he is responding he is watching the coach and trying to read his reaction. He probably expects to be in trouble since he didn't know the correct answer. But if the coach thought it was closer to a two, he would calmly reply, "I thought it was closer to a two." Seeing that there is no adverse consequence he tries again and responds with a more confident, "Three." As the drill progresses he becomes more confident with each answer because he realizes that there is no penalty for a wrong answer. If the coach agreed with the player's answer he says, "I agree." If he thought the movement didn't match the number, coach tells him, "I thought it was . . ." What happens very quickly, sometimes within ten shots or less, is that the player will begin moving toward the five position without the coach ever asking him to do so. He knew long ago that a five was the most efficient position but without consciously thinking about it he began shooting fours and fives consistently. Remember the goal was not for him to shoot a five but to know where his elbow was on each shot.

Sometimes movements can happen so quickly or be so complex that it is difficult to feel exactly what you did. If you are not able to feel what you have done, try listening to it! While coaching at Boston University and attending graduate school, I worked with an athlete named Declan Haggarty who was born and raised in Ireland but had found his way to Boston on an athletic scholarship. Declan was one of the best collegiate hammer throwers in the country. Both of us were enrolled in a course taught by one of the leading Motor Control & Learning experts in the country, Dr. Len Zaichkowsky. One of the topics we discussed at length was biofeedback. Declan and I started thinking about ways that we could apply what we were learning in class to improve athletic performance.

The hammer throw involves making no less than four high speed 360 degree turns in a seven foot circle while holding onto a sixteen pound ball connected to a four foot wire. Just watching it is a lesson in physics and when done well it is mesmerizing. Declan was having some difficulty mastering the depth and rhythm of the four turns during his throw. So with heads full of ideas we made our way over to the local Radio Shack to see what kind of electrical components we could find to improve his technique.

As the clerk put the nine volt battery and connector, buzzer device, and alligator clips into the bag the excitement grew. Next we headed over to the stationary store and bought two thin metal rulers with holes on the end of each and then we rummaged around our apartments for some small nuts and bolts, tape, and elastic wraps. Declan and I spent the afternoon building a biofeedback device that would beep when he dropped to the desired depth during each turn of his throw. We joined the rulers together with a nut and bolt, and aligned it on the side of his leg with the hinge in line with the center of his knee joint. We placed elastic wraps on his thigh and calf to hold the hinged apparatus in place. This was no small feat given that Declan had the biggest, strongest legs that I had ever seen. Finally, we secured the battery and buzzer to one of the rulers with tape and the electrical wires attached to alligator clips which could be positioned along the rulers to make contact with each other at any depth or angle. We were so excited about our invention that we immediately raced out to the throwing circle. The first time Declan threw with it on we heard nothing on the first turn and then, "Beep, beeep, beeeeeep" on the next three turns. The transformation within several throws was amazing. By the tenth throw we heard a sharp, "Beep, beep, beep, beep" in perfect timing. Within several weeks of using the makeshift device, Declan had one of the leading throws in the world! Awareness is the key. Knowing where you are in space by feeling, hearing, or touching is the secret to perfecting your technique.

REACTION TIME & SPEED

In the world of sport, speed is king. If you are fast you will go a long way on that ability alone. Consider that fortunes are made or lost on a forty yard time during the NFL Combine where the best collegiate football players across the country come to prove their athletic prowess to NFL teams. A wide-receiver who runs a 4.60 second forty-yard time is probably not going to play in the NFL but a receiver who runs a 4.50 second forty-yard time has a good chance. If that same player runs just one-tenth of a second faster, 4.40 seconds, he will probably become a top NFL draft pick and sign with a team for millions of dollars. One-tenth of a second! Take a handheld stop watch and try to start and stop it with your thumb or forefinger as fast as you can. Maybe three tenths of a second? Consider that you were not able to move your finger less than a sixteenth of an inch in three tenths of a second and yet entire careers are determined by one- or two-tenths of a second! The good news is that you can easily drop a tenth of a second, the bad news is you can just as easily add one if you don't know what you are doing.

A player doesn't need to look past the first six feet of his forty yard sprint to drop a tenth. Most players in a three point stance start position will push off with one leg and step with the other rather than initially pushing off with both legs. They will also tend to stand up too soon rather than firing straight out. They will also tend to pick up their hand too soon which starts the clock running rather than keeping their support hand on the ground as long as possible while they push off with both legs. These subtle differences will easily save a tenth of a second and possibly millions of dollars!

Technique, however, is only part of the solution to becoming really fast. Your body only moves as fast as your mind wills it. To demonstrate, try snapping your finger fast one time now. No, I mean really fast. Try it one more time as you say, "Go!" You were probably faster than the first time but you have more to give. Pinch your cheeks, wake up, bring up as much energy as you can muster. Imagine a loud alarm has just sounded. Try snapping your finger as fast as you can again but be aware that you have been most likely waiting for the whole "Go!" to come out before moving. This time listen carefully and try to snap your finger on the first utterance of the "g" sound, "guh." Ready? Go! Guaranteed that was faster than both the other tries. Ask yourself, "Why didn't I snap it that fast the first time?" You might say, "Well, I didn't really know you meant that fast or I didn't know that I could even move that fast." Combining great technique with mental quickness is the secret to maximizing your speed.

STRENGTH—MENTAL AND PHYSICAL

If world-class speed has a mental component then so does strength. I have demonstrated this fact hundreds of times at presentations around the country but on one of those occasions something happened that scared me. Usually I ask for a volunteer to come up on stage to demonstrate how feats of peak performance strength can occur. Typically a young athletic male or female will jump up and volunteer but one time, before I knew what was happening, an eighty year old woman came up to the stage. Everyone applauded and I thought, "This should be interesting." Her name was Gertrude and I asked her to extend her arm straight out in front of her with her palm facing up and then to make a tight fist. I told Gertrude, "I'm going to try to bend your arm and I want you to try and stop me from doing it." I placed my left forearm against her biceps (front upper arm) just above the elbow joint, grabbed her wrist with my right hand, and began pushing down with my forearm and up with my hand, trying to move her forearm upwards. It didn't take much force before her forearm began to move. I kept moving her arm until her elbow was at about a ninety degree angle. I congratulated her on her effort but it was apparent to the audience that her arm gave way fairly easily.

Then I directed her attention to a corner of the ballroom ceiling and had her stretch out her arm in the same way except it was pointed at that spot on the ceiling with her hand opened rather than in a fist. I said, "Gertrude, imagine that you see smoke coming out of the ceiling. There is a fire raging behind the panels and it is ready to burst out. Picture a fire hose in action and the immense power of the water shooting out through the nozzle. Imagine your arm is the hose, with hundreds of pounds of pressure rocketing the water through it onto the ceiling." I moved my hand along the length of her arm, wrist, and hand several times in the direction of the "fire" and I repeated, "hundreds of pounds of pressure, hundreds of pounds of pressure. See the fire. Keep focused on the fire, keep the water on it." Gertrude was completely absorbed in putting out the fire. While I continue to repeat the words, "Hundreds of pounds of pressure, hundreds of pounds of pressure," I placed my left forearm on her biceps and right hand on her wrist and began to push.

I gradually applied pressure in ever increasing amounts until I was pushing with all of my might. But Gertrude's arm didn't budge an inch. I was shaking as I applied full pressure to her arm and wrist in an attempt to bend her arm at the elbow. This is when I got scared. I suddenly became aware that I was applying an incredible amount of force to an eighty-year-old woman's arm and that at any second one of her bones might snap in half! I stopped instantly, relieved that Gertrude's upper arm was still in one piece. The audience looked in amazement as I asked Gertrude, "Could you feel how hard I was pressing?" She said, "Yes, but it really didn't seem to matter. I was trying to put out the fire!" I continued, "But how did you do it? How did you suddenly get so much stronger?" Gertrude wasn't sure how she had done it, but obviously, something happened. It was Gertrude's arm in both cases, the same bones and muscles. The answer, in part, is that she helped bend her own arm the first time.

By trying to stop me from bending her arm Gertrude inadvertently contracted all of her arm muscles including her biceps which is the primary muscle group used to flex or bend an arm. However, the second time Gertrude was not distracted or concerned about her arm being bent because she was intent on putting out the fire. She did two things that led to her peak performance. She was completely focused on the task at hand, and she only used the muscles, her triceps, necessary to lock out her arm. The combination of being absorbed in the details, better known as being "in the zone," and contracting only the muscles necessary for the task resulted in her amazing performance. If Gertrude could demonstrate this kind of Herculean strength, what are you capable of doing?

Aside from the mental aspects of strength are the physiological factors that determine the force and power of your movements. Athletic strength is not just a matter of going into the gym and lifting huge amounts of weight. Although the strongest people in the world can lift very heavy weights, that does not always make them the best or strongest athlete on the field. The secret is not in the absolute weight you can lift but in how fast you can generate the force necessary for the task at hand. If you can only squat 250 pounds and your competitor can squat over 500 pounds it would seem that he has the advantage. However, if jumping for a rebound requires generating 250 pounds of force in 0.2 seconds and you can generate it in 0.1 seconds while your stronger competitor can only generate the same 250 pounds of force in 0.3 seconds, you will win every time. You can gain this advantage by incorporating strength and power drills that require very short ground contact times in your training.

The way you ensure that you will maximize your strength, power, flexibility, and technique is by using a periodized training program. That means the type of work you do is varied over time so that it culminates with a period that enables you to perform at your very best during the peak of your season. For example, if you do the same number of set and reps for the bench press and continually try to increase the weight every time you lift, you will plateau and become stale. Instead of repeating 3 sets of 10 reps indefinitely, you might do three weeks at 5 sets of 8 reps, then three weeks at 5 sets of 5 reps, then three weeks at 5 sets of 3 reps, and then two weeks at 3 sets of 3 reps. Each week you vary the weight lifted along a heavy, medium, light format that is also varied (i.e., week one: light, medium, heavy; week two: medium, light, heavy; week three: light, heavy, medium; etc.). Each week you will notice that you are able to lift more weight on your heavy day. In this way you will continually get stronger and see your performance improve from week to week. Periodized training is the foundation of every Olympian and world-class athlete's top performance and it is the only way to go if you want to ensure that your time in the gym is well spent.

Preparation & Training for Peak Performance

If you are not improving in some way each day there is something wrong with what you are doing. Many athletes go to practice each day and, without realizing it, go through the motions of practicing a skill without ever getting any better at it. This is a waste of time that can easily be eliminated by knowing in detail what you are trying to improve and then focusing on the skills necessary to master it. Instead of an NFL wide receiver running route after route and catching eight out of ten balls, he should be asking, "Why am I not catching the ninth or tenth?" You might say, "Well, isn't that normal? After all, he is only human. He is going to drop some balls every once and a while." Of course that is true but he should be trying to minimize the number of balls he drops, not just accepting that a dropped ball is inevitable.

Unless he gives his 100 percent he will never know. There is always a reason why a ball is dropped and in the case of an NFL wide receiver it isn't because he can't catch. Knowing what he did on every play is essential to catching the tenth ball. Is he seeing the ball in detail? Or does he see the ball as a blurry brown thing flying through the air, rather than seeing the details of seams and laces? Practice may start by holding a football in his hands and looking at the tip of the ball where the seams come together to form a cross. During practice or a game his desire to see the cross, will help him to see the ball better and make the catch. Perhaps he sees the ball in detail but doesn't snap his head around fast enough to see the ball coming before it is on top of him? Or does his head sweep around, blurring the image and lengthening the time before he sees the ball rather than instantly snapping it around as he plants to cut? It is the difference between him seeing a ball fifteen feet sooner or experiencing the shock of suddenly being hit in his face mask. Maybe he sees a ball in detail and his head snaps around but does he watch the ball until his fingers close in around it? Or does he watch the ball until it is about a foot away and then begin looking up field rather than watching the ball stick in his hands? You can catch a lot of balls with your peripheral vision but that is not how he will catch ten out of ten. Even if he does these three things he can still drop a ball if the ball has energy greater than his hands. If a ball is coming in at 60mph then he needs to take the ball with energy greater than 60mph otherwise there is a good chance that it will sail right through his hands. Often if a player waits for a fast ball to hit his outstretched hands, or tries to body catch it, he will drop the ball. During practice he can overcome this problem by "taking" the ball out of the air rather than passively waiting for it to hit him. Even if the receiver was able to master these four things, the next challenge would be to increase his mental and physical endurance to do it on every ball without fatiguing or losing focus.

BLOCKING OUT DISTRACTIONS

Leif Smith, an experienced sports psychologist, often talks about athletes and their mental rituals. Whether you want to call them mental rituals or cues or triggers, they are, in essence, techniques that help you get ready mentally for performing the task at hand. Dr. Smith points out that you can often see examples of these mental rituals in tennis tournaments. Between serves, many players bounce around on the balls of their feet with their hands on their rackets and appear to be adjusting the strings with their fingers. That action helps to keep their focus on the task at hand instead of allowing their minds to wander to such things as, "What will the next serve look like?" or "Where will it go and will I be able to return it?" Although focusing on fixing the strings on your racket isn't necessarily preparing you to see the next ball, it is helping to block out all the distractions between points. To this end, Dr. Smith also suggests having a place or movement that allows you to regroup. He recommends that when players lose a particularly difficult point or become distracted that they go to their towel behind the baseline to renew and collect themselves. He believes that by doing this, players are conditioned to regain their focus quickly whenever they go to their towel.

Another simple technique that will also help you to block out distractions and perform at your best takes less than ten seconds. Any time you feel upset or agitated try thinking, "Oh God, come to my assistance," and center yourself. You can do this by taking in a full deep breath, holding it for a second or two, and then letting it out very slowly while feeling gravity pull your entire center of gravity toward the floor. Over time you will become so proficient at it that you will be able to relax in the middle of a crowd and no one will know it, except you!

PUTTING IT ALL TOGETHER

Have you ever said, "Oh! Wait, I wasn't ready, " or "Hey, that's not suppose to happen," or "I could've gotten that one if . . ." You might still be able to hear the lament of a childhood friend who cries out, "Do over!" Preparing for the unexpected is preparing for peak performance. Since you don't know when the tipped ball will suddenly be within your grasp, the only way to ensure that you will be ready to catch it is by committing 100 percent of all your skill, talents, and abilities to the task at hand in the present moment. That includes using the physical attributes of strength, power, speed, and skill as well as the mental ability to become so absorbed in the details that time ceases to exist. Putting all of it together in a game or competition provides the opportunity for peak performance and the joy and wonder that comes from being part of something special.

For one NFL tight end the acronym PTASE, which I made up, was the key to unlocking many peak performances and becoming one of the best blocking tight ends in the game. Kyle Brady had signed with the Jacksonville Jaguars as the highest paid tight end in the NFL. Kyle was already considered a great blocking tight end but he was looking for something more. He wasn't satisfied with being the best blocking tight end; he wanted to know that he was making the ultimate block on every play. Although it didn't happen often, he would occasionally be out of position or miss a block. Others might have written them off as an anomaly but not Kyle. PTASE was the way he ensured that each block would be his best. It stands for: **P**lay, **T**arget, **A**ction, **S**pot, and **E**nergy.

"P" meant knowing every play instantaneously in the huddle. Think of how long it takes you to answer this question, "What's your name?" That is how fast he came to recognize even the most complex plays including audibles at the line of scrimmage. "T" was knowing the player that he would have primary responsibility for blocking. "A" reminded him the direction the play would be running. This was particularly helpful when he had to go in motion and stop in front of the player he had to block. For instance if the play was running to the inside he knew to line up just a hair inside of the center line of the player to be blocked. This made all the difference in the world in his ability to quickly step to shield off the inside once the ball was snapped. "S" meant that instead of reacting with a pre-scripted movement or trying to take in all of the players' gyrations and moves, Kyle would focus in great detail on one specific spot on the player's jersey. That spot could never fake him out. "E" required playing with maximum intensity until the whistle blew. Instead of just one initial burst of energy that would gradually fade over the course of the play, Kyle's blocking at the end of a play was indistinguishable from the way it began.

One particular instance shows the power of Kyle's PTASE strategy. According to the *Jacksonville Times-Union* newspaper, the result was a peak performance against Peyton Manning's Indianapolis Colts.

> [Dwight] Freeney, a fearsome pass-rush specialist for the Indianapolis Colts with a knack for forcing fumbles, loomed as a potential nightmare Sunday for the fumble-prone Leftwich. Freeney came in with six sacks and three forced fumbles in his previous three games, including three sacks and two forced fumbles the week before in a 23-17 victory at Miami. But with Pearson getting blocking help on almost every pass play from tight end Kyle Brady or a running back, Freeney never got close enough to bat the ball out of Leftwich's hands. "The offensive line did a heck of a job," Leftwich said. "All week, we heard about their defensive line, but it was our offensive line that held the fort and made this win possible." Specifically, the Jaguars held the fort against Freeney, making it impossible for the NFL's hottest sack artist the past three weeks to put pressure on Leftwich (*Times-Union*).

PTASE allowed Kyle to stop one of the best defensive ends in the NFL and open up holes in the defensive line that you could drive a bus through. It also enabled him to manipulate the players on the field into moving out of position when he was running pass routes. The result was Kyle's ability to consistently get the first down or score in key situations. He used PTASE with great success throughout his career with Jacksonville and brought it to bear in his final season with the New England Patriots by helping them to go undefeated in the regular season. "To me, a game is all about playing one play at a time," Brady said. That may sound overly clichéd, but you can't control the final outcome when you're stepping on the field for the first play of the game. All you can control is that particular play, what you do on that particular play, how well you execute that particular play. When the thirteen year veteran was asked if he felt any pressure, he said, "There are far better things to focus on than a self-generated pressure and its potential consequences." Years of perfecting PTASE led him to say, "The best thing to focus on is what you are doing in the here-and-now, beginning with hearing the play in the huddle. If you focus in that way, the outcome will take care of itself."

In golf, the PTASE equivalent is playing "ball-to-ball." It is an extremely effective way to improve your golf game and it has been successfully used by high handicappers as well as by tour winners. Playing ball-to-ball involves doing three things on every shot or putt. First, see the target. Imagine that you are standing on the first tee ready to hit your ball. Instead of thinking about all of the "hazards" and hundreds of instructions that typically run through your mind, simply look down the fairway. Instantly, within a hundredth of a second, your eye will go to the target or ideal spot. If you are not aware of your first glance, then you will probably continue to study the fairway which will cause you to guess or deduce where the ideal spot is located. More often than not you will be wrong. Trust your brain's ability to see the best one. "But what if it is very windy?" you might say. What if it is? Do you think your brain did not register the wind? Do you think you needed to tell your brain that it is windy out and that it better start making adjustments? No, your brain has taken it all in and quickly identified the perfect spot. Go with it. Secondly, feel your body. Take a practice swing that you believe will put your ball on that ideal spot. Immediately step up to your ball. Third, see the ball. Not a white fuzzy thing but the speck or mark on the ball that you will hit. Bore in on that detail as you begin your swing by trying to see the speck within the speck. Once you have hit the ball the first thing that should register with you is, "Was that my practice swing?" Yes or no. If yes, no comments out loud or in your mind. Walk on to your next ball. If no, "How was it different?" Don't answer with words. *Feel* what you did differently between the practice swing and the actual swing. Once you have it, walk on with no further comment inside or outside of your head. When you reach your ball, you repeat exactly the same steps. See your target, feel your body, and then see the ball. After that shot ask the same question, "Was that my practice swing?" If yes, move on, if no, feel the difference between the practice and actual swing and then move on to your next shot. Repeat that ball after ball after ball until they tell you to stop playing. You no longer play golf, you play ball-to-ball.

In golf the score is all that counts. In ball-to-ball complete focus and absorption in the details and your ability to feel what you did is all that counts. Ironically, playing ball-to-ball lowers your score! By pulling together the unique components of performance that you have learned and practiced, you will find your own PTASE or ball-to-ball equivalent. It is when you can finally take the complex and make it simple that peak performances become commonplace.

TAKE AWAY

Peak performances are the result of intense focus on the task at hand in the present moment. The more absorbed you become in the details of any activity the more likely a peak performance will occur. Perfecting your technique requires effective physical training and the ability to precisely feel what you did during your actual performance. By improving your ability to feel the subtlest differences in your movements, you will be able to choose the one that results in your best performance.

PART THREE

PLAYING WITH A PASSION THAT NEVER ENDS

CHAPTER 8

O Captain! My Captain!

I T IS often said, "Some people are born to lead," but it is those who possess virtue and are willing to make the ultimate sacrifice that inspire us to do the same. When the time comes, usually unexpectedly, will you be ready and willing to answer the call without hesitation, to give your all?

There are countless stories about individuals who have risked or sacrificed their lives for their neighbor or their country, but one that stands out is about a very ordinary man who did a very extraordinary thing. It was the winter of 1982 and Air Florida Flight 90 had just taken off from Washington National Airport when it crashed into the 14th Street Bridge and plunged into the frozen Potomac River. The blizzard-like conditions made it nearly impossible for rescue workers to get to the crash site and the few that did were not able to reach the near frozen victims. The ice was unstable and there was no way to reach the survivors. All the bystanders could do was yell words of encouragement and wait for the rescuers to arrive.

Finally, a forest service helicopter, not designed for water rescue, appeared and its crew desperately worked to pull the few survivors from the thirty-three degree water. At that temperature a person can only survive for about thirty minutes. But there was one passenger they couldn't help. Blinded by jet fuel and quickly succumbing to the freezing water, Priscilla Tirado struggled to keep her face above the surface. She was about to die.

By now hundreds of people lined the shore and bridges watching Priscilla, the last survivor of the crash, fight for her life. While this tragedy was unfolding, a man by the name of Lenny Skutnik, a mail room clerk who was on his way home from work, stopped to see what was happening. He stood there for a moment watching Priscilla. He said, "The hair stood up on the back of my neck and I knew that I could not just stand there and watch her die. I had to try to do something." With that thought he ripped off his coat, boots, and with short sleeves, dove into the icy water and swam to Priscilla who was just going under for the last time. Lenny grabbed her and managed to drag her to the rescue workers. He had instant hypothermia and was taken to a waiting ambulance when he got to the river bank. If the rescue didn't already tell you all you needed to know about Lenny Skutnik then his act of selflessness in the back of that ambulance will. While in the ambulance he saw a crash victim with two broken legs who was shivering and gave this person his coat. (To see the actual footage of the rescue go to YouTube and search, "Ordinary Heroes—Lenny Skutnik.")

If virtue is the habit of doing good, then Lenny must have had a lot of practice! He was a regular person, living an ordinary life. He didn't calculate the risk. He saw someone in desperate need and acted. We might never find ourselves in a life or death situation but we are called to the same heroic virtue whether it's at work, at home, or on the field of play.

What is at the root of this kind of heroic virtue and great leadership? What brings a man to risk his life by jumping into deathly cold water to rescue a complete stranger? Money, power, fame? The cynic would say, "Yes, probably all three!" It is none of these. I know it may sound too simple but it's love. Yeah, love,

love, love. I know what you might be thinking, oh no a sport book disguised as a love book! But love is the most motivating force in sport, business and everyday life and I'll prove it.

What if I said, "I'll give you a billion dollars and make you the president. The only stipulation is that you'll have to live on a deserted island for the rest of your life." Are you going to take that deal? Nobody is going to take that deal. Now, you may be feeling a bit exhausted with life and you might even enjoy a couple of weeks on the island but you would not want to stay there alone for the rest of your life! If money, power, or fame were truly the most motivating things, we would say, "Yeah! Yeah, I'll take it. That's fantastic; it's everything I've always wanted. In fact it's the thing I want most in life . . . and now I have it. I'll be very happy forever on my deserted island." But we don't say that. The reason is that what we really want, even more than money, power, or fame—what we're really hoping to get—is love. We wouldn't want to stay on the deserted island because there are no people. And without people, there is no potential for relationships and love. So love is the most motivating thing to you and me and everyone else in the world.

Well another word for love is sacrifice. Sacrifice means, "I'm willing to do something for you. I'm willing to give up something that I could keep for myself in order to give it to you." It's about this idea of "otherness". . ."I'm focused on you. I love you. I want the most for you." That means everyone, teammate, co-worker, family member or friend. Love is literally more essential to our happiness and well-being than the air we breathe. It is also the secret to true and lasting success and happiness in sport, business and everyday life. If you are freed up to love those around you, you will never stand alone.

Love is ever present in sport but rarely talked about. It is the underlying reason for such fierce loyalty and strong bonds of friendship among teammates and competitors regardless of socioeconomic, political or religious differences. Perhaps there is no more dramatic example of this than between Jesse Owens and Luz Long.

In 1936 Jesse Owens was perhaps the most recognized man in the world, and yet he struggled to be seen for who he really was. As one of the greatest track and field athletes of all-time, he is best known for his four-gold-medal performance at the 1936 Berlin Olympic Games where he single handedly destroyed Adolf Hitler's claim of Aryan superiority. What makes the story all the more remarkable is the fact that a young German athlete wearing a Nazi swastika on his uniform helped him to do it.

One year prior to the Olympic Games, Jesse turned the track and field world on its head by breaking three world records (220 yards, 220 yard Hurdles, and Long Jump) and tying a fourth (100 yards) at the Big Ten Championships in the span of forty-five minutes. His long jump record—26' 8.16"—would stand for over twenty-five years.

Just one year later he stood on the long jump runway in Berlin ready to leap his way to his second gold medal of the Games. As part of his customary warm-up, he sprinted down the runway and then ran through the sand landing pit only to turn around to see a red flag waving, indicating a foul. Apparently the custom of running through the pit was a U.S. invention and not permitted at the Games. This rattled Jesse to the point that on his next jump he was so concerned about missing the take-off board and fouling again that he chopped his steps before take-off and only jumped 23' 3" which was two inches short of distance needed to qualify for the finals. He was down to his last jump and described the mounting anxiety that threatened to end his chance of making the finals. "What if I, I stopped myself from thinking it time and again, but it kept crashing through my mind, what if, what if, . . . what if I didn't qualify? Hitler won't look so crazy, then . . .

I fought, fought hard, harder but one cell at a time, panic crept into my body."

In his autobiography *Jesse, The Man Who Outran Hitler*, he wrote:

> I walked back to the broad-jump area. As I did, I heard
> a name called. Mine. Now it was my turn. I have to find
> strength somewhere, I said to myself. Have to reach into
> myself and find the strength to make it, to do my best.
> Almost instinctively, I began to drop down on my knees.
> Pray. Must pray, I whispered to myself. But in front of
> a hundred thousand people? "Jesse Owens!" It was the
> loudspeaker announcing my name for the second time.
> I closed my eyes, one of my knees touching the ground.
> Oh, God, I pleaded wordlessly with everything that was
> inside me. Help me to pray. But I couldn't. Couldn't.
> "Jesse Owens!" They were calling my name for the last
> time. I had to get up, jump. But I hadn't prayed. "Jesse
> Owens!" Suddenly I felt a hand on my shoulder. It wasn't
> the loudspeaker calling my name a final time. It was a
> man standing right there next to me.

At that moment Jesse heard a voice from behind him offer some kindly advice. Jesse turned to see the German long jump champion Luz Long. Owens described the moment:

> The way his hand rested on my shoulder, the vibrations I
> felt as he looked at me and smiled, made me know some-
> how that, far from being my enemy, he was my friend.
> "I Luz Long," he said, introducing himself. I nodded. "I
> think I know what is wrong with you," he went on. "You
> give everything when you jump. I the same. You can-
> not do halfway, but you are afraid you will foul again."
> "That's right," I said, finding my voice for the first time.

"I have answer," he said. "Same thing happen to me last year in Cologne." There were literally only seconds left before I had to jump or default. Luz told me to simply remeasure my steps and jump from six inches in back of the takeoff board—giving it all I had. That way I could give 100 percent, and still not be afraid of fouling. He even laid his towel down at exactly the place from which I was to jump.

It was so simple! Amazingly Jesse took off almost a foot behind the board and still jumped twenty-five feet. He was in the finals!

Jesse was overwhelmed with gratitude for the incredible act of sportsmanship shown by Luz. From that point on they became fast friends and they spent most of that evening, extending well into the night, drinking coffee and talking about track and life. At one point the conversation drifted to religion and Jesse asked Luz, "Do you believe in God?" Luz replied with a shrug of his shoulders and a slight tilt of his head as if to say, "I don't know." Jesse later recalled, "Even though he [Luz] didn't believe in God, I believed in Luz Long. We spent each night afterward talking, and the days competing."

The long jump final proved no less exciting than the qualifying round but in a different way. With three jumps each in the final round, Luz and Jesse traded new Olympic records five times during the competition. As Jesse leaped out of the pit on the last jump of the competition the first person to reach him was Luz. He said, "You did it! I know you did it." And he was right. Jesse had won the competition on the final jump and set a new Olympic games record of 26' 5.25".

Jesse said:

> Luz Long may not have believed in God, but God had believed in Luz Long. And God had sent him to me.

You can melt down all the gold medals and cups I have, and they wouldn't be a plating on the 24-carat friendship I felt for Luz Long at that moment. I realized then, too, that Luz was the epitome of what Pierre de Coubertin, founder of the modern Olympic Games, must have had in mind when he said, 'The important thing in the Olympic Games is not winning but taking part. The essential thing in life is not conquering but fighting well.' Though neither of us imagined it then, that would be the last time we would see each other. The dark tides of politics and war were to pull us forever apart. Still we had become brothers in that one perfect moment of competition and charity. We vowed to correspond.

"For a while I was one of the most famous people on earth," noted Jesse. He had arrived back in the United States to a hero's welcome including a ticker-tape parade down Fifth Avenue in New York City. However, he quickly learned that his accomplishment was welcomed but not Jesse, the man of color. As he approached the Waldorf Astoria Hotel where the banquet in his honor was being held that evening, he was required to use the rear entrance and take the freight elevator to the dinner. In his own words, "I soon discovered how empty fame can be, and how easily it could be exploited by those who would use it, and me, for gain. I became entangled in a number of bad business deals and in a few years, I was bankrupt. It was only the steadfastness of my family and the friendship of Luz Long expressed in letters that helped me through."

Jesse related:

Luz was undergoing trials, too. Germany had plunged into war, and he was in the military. After a while the letters we had faithfully exchanged every month or two stopped altogether. Soon America was in the war. I joined up. And then one day I received a letter posted from North Africa. It was over a year old. It was from Luz. It said, in part:

"I am here, Jesse, where it seems there is only the dry sand and the wet blood. My heart tells me, if I be honest with you, that this is the last letter I shall ever write. That hour in Berlin when I first spoke to you, when you had your knee upon the ground, I knew that you were in prayer. And I know it is never by chance that we come together. And you, I believe, will read this letter. I believe this shall come about because I think now that God will make it come about. This is what I have to tell you, Jesse. I believe in God. And I pray to Him that, even while it should not be possible to see you again, these words I write will still be read by you. Your brother, Luz."

Those were Luz's last words. I learned shortly thereafter that he had been killed in battle just a few days after he had written his letter to me. Our friendship had proved greater than the forces which divided our nations. I had not lost my brother. His letter spoke the truth: . . . it is never by chance that we come together. God had sent him to me at a moment of personal despair, and he brought me the gift of hope. Bowing, but unable to pray on that Olympic field, I had given him a sign, a seed of faith which was to blossom in the deserts of North Africa. Together we had shared the greatest gift of all, which comes from God. The gift of brotherly love which neither competition, nor war, nor even death could annul." (Excerpted from *Jesse, The Man Who Outran Hitler*, by Jesse Owens and Paul Neimark. Published by Logos International, Plainfield, N.J., 1978. Used with permission.)

Just like their friendship, the story didn't end there. Many years later, Jesse received a letter from Luz Long's son, Kyle, who was then twenty-two-years old and getting married. The letter read, "Even though my father can't be here to be my best man, I know who he would want in his place. He would want someone that he and his entire family admired and respected. He would want you to take his place. And I do, too." Jesse Owens flew to Germany to be the best man at Kyle's wedding. Jesse once said, "Friendships are born on the field of athletic strife and are the real gold of competition. Awards become corroded, friends gather no dust." He was a man of his word.

Perhaps the greatest example of love in action in the world of sport and life is that of Amos Alonzo Stagg. His whole life was devoted to the habit of doing good. To perfecting all that he had been given. Remember the parable of the servant who was given five talents and then found a way to double them? That is Amos Alonzo Stagg. His life inspires generation after generation to do more, to give more, and to be more.

How does a man five feet six inches tall, weighing one-hundred and fifty pounds dripping wet, become one of the greatest football players and coaches of all-time? The simple answer is that you can't judge a book by its cover. The more complex answer is that Amos Alonzo Stagg was a deep well. He was one of those rare people who double their talents by integrating the physical, mental, and spiritual in all that they do. In his late teens he developed into an extraordinary pitcher. He received numerous offers from professional teams such as the New York Giants to play baseball. To the disbelief of his teammates and friends, he declined the offers to play professionally and headed to Yale Divinity School where he hoped to become a minister. It turned out that Yale had a baseball team and a football team and both of them were only too glad to welcome Amos to their ranks. He ended up leading the Yale Baseball Team to five Championships (it was permissible at the time to compete for a fifth year while completing a Masters Degree) and was a member of arguably one of the greatest football teams of all-time which in 1888 went undefeated and un-scored upon (698-0).

Given Amos's strong desire to be a minister it is not surprising that he came to be known for his virtue, especially as it applied to sport. Unfortunately he lacked one essential thing a preacher needs: the ability to preach. He was soft spoken, struggled to express himself in front of large audiences, and as he noted, "stammered terribly." This revelation led him to the Springfield Training School (YMCA) where he coached and captained the football team. Ironically, James Naismith, the founder of basketball, was the starting center on his football team. Before leaving Springfield for the University of Chicago two years later, Amos played in the first public game of basketball—students versus teachers—and scored the only point for his team in an extremely low scoring 5-to-1 loss. For his early involvement and his many later contributions to the game, he would be inducted into the Naismith Memorial Basketball Hall of Fame in 1958.

His decision to leave Springfield was about something much deeper than money, prestige or position. In reply to William Rainey Harper, the president of the University of Chicago, Amos wrote, "After much thought and prayer I have decided that my life can be best used for my Master's Service in the position you have offered." Although he would not be preaching from the pulpit, he came to realize that, "I felt specially called to preach but I decided to do it on the athletic fields!" Upon his arrival at the University of Chicago, he was appointed the director of the department of physical culture and the head football coach. He held these positions for over forty years and won two National Championships and seven Big Ten Championships. Amos was an innovator and inventor. He introduced the QB sneak, "T" formation, man in motion, onside kick, lateral pass, huddle,

Statue of Liberty play, quick kick, reverse, and many more. On the day the forward pass became legal in 1906 he already had sixty-four plays ready to go. He created hip pads, tackling dummies and padded goal posts, and he was the first to employ numbered jerseys.

During his tenure at the University of Chicago he also managed to coach the baseball team for seventeen years and create the first batting cage. Nothing seemed beyond the scope of his fertile imagination. He even invented the first trough for swimming pools to reduce turbulence and decrease the water overflow. As if he wasn't busy enough, he also coached the track team for thirty-two years and he was selected to coach the 400m and 800m runners on the 1924 United States Olympic track team in Paris. He continued as a member of the U.S. Olympic Committee for six Olympiads and chaired the NCAA Championships for twelve years.

Despite all of these incredible accomplishments, Amos Alonzo Stagg was best known for his character and integrity. His reputation for honesty and fair play was legendary. On two separate occasions, when referees did not show up for a football game that his team was playing in, the opposing team asked Amos to referee the games. Virtue was his secret to a good and happy life. He expected everyone of his charges to live this way and even created the varsity letter system in order to recognize those players who did. He awarded a letter based on a young man "qualifying for manhood" and not exclusively on his ability as an athlete. In his book on sports virtue entitled *Amos Alonzo Stagg*, Fritz Knapp wrote, "Some of his better players did not earn letters, and he honestly confronted them with the truth when they hadn't shown the kind of spirit that he looked for in a letterman, namely 'faithfulness to practice and the rules of training, fidelity to fair play and good sportsmanship, and loyalty to the athletic ideals of the University.'"

By living the ideals that he preached to others, Amos earned the undying love and respect of all who knew him. In 1951 he would become the first person inducted into the College Football Hall of Fame as both a player and a coach. Some think that perhaps Notre Dame's Knute Rockne best summed it up when he said, "All of football comes from Stagg," but Amos found that by being faithful and pursuing the truth first, the victories on and off the field always seemed to follow. As Mother Theresa often said, "I am not called to be successful, but to be faithful."

Stories about his moral character and love for each of his players are endless. After observing the kids tearing up Amos's pristine lawn each day while playing football, a neighbor approached him and said, "You'll never raise grass that way." To which Amos quickly shot back, "I'm not raising grass. I'm raising boys!" Another time after one particularly fine season, a reporter asked Coach Stagg, "Coach, was this your most successful team?" Stagg replied, "I won't know that for another 20 or 30 years."

Perhaps no story could better capture the essence of the man than the letter he wrote to his one-year-old son, Amos Jr., expressing his love and offering him advice on how to live a good life and be happy.

> To My Son,
> June 23, 1900
>
> You're only a little fellow now—a trifle over 14 months old; but I have loved you so dearly since you came that it has been on my mind to write you a letter in the event of my being taken away at any time before I had a chance to tell you many things which you need to know.
>
> Your father wants his Boy first of all to love, protect, and care for his Mother, giving to her the same kind of measure of love and devotion which she has given to you.

Second, your father wants his Boy to be sincere, honest and upright and be your truest self always. Hate dishonesty and trickery no matter how big and how great the thing desired may be.

Third, your father wants you to have a proper independence of thought. Think matters out for yourself always where it relates to your own conduct and act honestly afterwards.

Fourth, your father wants you to be an American in democracy. Treat everybody with courtesy and as your equal until he proves his unworthiness to be so treated. The man and the soul are what counts and not wealth, not family, not appearance.

Fifth, your father wants you to abhor evil. No curiosity, no imagination, no conversation, no story, no reading which suggests impurity of life is worthy of your thought, or attention and I beg you never to yield for an instant but turn your thought to something good and helpful.

Sixth, train yourself to be master of yourself, of your thought and imagination and temper and passion and appetite and of your body. Allow no thought, nor imagination, nor passion, nor appetite to injure your mind or body. Your father has never used intoxicating liquors, nor tobacco, nor profane language. He wants his Boy to be like him in this regard.

Seventh, your father wants his Boy enthusiastic and earnest in all of his interests, his sports, his studies, his work; he wants him always to keep an active, actual participation in each so long as he lives. It is my judgment that one's life is most healthy and most successful when lived on such a basis.

Eighth, your father wants his son to love God as He

is revealed to him; which after all will be the revelation of all that I have said and left unsaid of good to you, my precious Boy.

Affectionately,
Your father,
Amos Alonzo Stagg

He was as good a father as he was a coach and as you might have imagined his marriage wasn't anything less. Stella, his wife, was a real character and loved him so deeply that she jumped into football with both feet. In a 1962 Sports Illustrated article, John Underwood wrote,

> Stella Stagg learned to diagram plays and to scout opponents, and to make his utilitarian meals palatable for the family. Once he showed her a new play he was going to spring on a COP opponent. She quickly worked out a defense for it. "That'll stop your play," she said. Stagg scratched his white head, puzzling. He padded off to the kitchen for a glass of water. Finally he returned. "He had a gleam in his eye and an eraser in his hand," says Mrs. Stagg. "You can't stop it now," he said with triumph, and erased one of my players. "You were using 12 men."

With her at his side, Amos at the age of eighty-one was named the 1943 National Football Coach of the Year over Frank Leahy of Notre Dame. Amos would continue to coach until he was ninety-six years old. Fifty-seven years as a head coach with a record of 314-199-35 and six years as an assistant for his son Amos Jr. at Susquehanna University and finally six years as the punting coach at Stockton College.

On his one hundredth birthday Amos was asked, "What do you think your legacy will be?" He replied thoughtfully as if he were already far away, "I would . . . like to be remembered . . .

as an honest man." In a birthday tribute, President John F. Kennedy wrote, "His character and career have been an inspiration since his undergraduate days for countless Americans. Few men in our history have set so persuasive and shining examples as a teacher, coach and citizen. His integrity and dedication to all the goals he has set for himself are unmatched." Amos and Stella were happily married for seventy years and somehow it seems fitting that they would both die within six months of each other. Amos was one-hundred and two years old.

Take Away

It's never too late. Whether you excel in one particular virtue like world-class athletic performance or academic excellence or business success, you are called to practice all of the virtues in all that you do. Your complete happiness depends on it. You are called to be a saint, to give your all—in mind, heart, body and soul. You are not called to be successful, but to be faithful. Are you attentive to the will of God in all aspects of your life? Being so, sooner than later, will prevent a lot of heartache and pain for you, your family, and those around you, and result in a life well-lived.

Faith, reason and a lifetime of preparation and dedication can prepare you to instantly recognize and respond to the most important moments of your life. These are the moments, if acted upon, that you will always cherish, and they are the ones that will be remembered by your children and your children's children. But this all comes at a price, a sacrifice. The question is, can you take it? Will you take it?

CHAPTER 9

PLAYING HURT

E VERY athlete has had to deal with pain from injury or pain
from the sacrifice required to train and compete at the
highest level. But pain is just a word. Reading it doesn't trigger
your pain receptors to fire. Remembering the time that your finger was smashed between two helmets or caught in the car door
is not the same as experiencing the actual pain at the instant it
occurs. But when it does happen, will you be able to take it? Will
you be able to take the pain and discomfort that may be required
to achieve your goals and aspirations?

Imagine that someone whom you love is sitting in a chair
across the room from you. It's someone you love so much that
you would die for them. Do you have this person in mind? Now
imagine that suddenly their chair bursts into flames. Would you
run over and pull that person off the chair? Most people would
say, "yes." What if I tell you that you'll be burned badly, right
down to your wrist bones? Would you still do it? Most people
still say, "Yes. Absolutely, it's someone I would die for."

Now imagine that I pull out a flamethrower and blast your
wrists with it. Burn you right down to the bones. You're going
to go nuts. You're going to roll around on the floor writhing
in pain, attack me, or run out of the room screaming. Same

burn, same pain as when you pulled the person off the burning chair. One you can take, the other you can't. Why? Because pain without purpose is intolerable. We can't take it. This is why it's so important to reflect on the question, "What is my purpose? What is a sufficiently compelling reason that would enable me to take the pain and sacrifice that I will be faced with in life?" If the answer isn't clear to you, you won't be able to take it when it comes. And it is coming!

C.S. Lewis explains why it is necessary that it does come. In his book, *Virtue and Vice*, he writes about tribulation as a necessary medicine for our welfare. Contrary to our human inclinations for comfort and ease, he makes a compelling case for tribulation as a mercy when he wrote:

> I am progressing along the path of life in my ordinary contentedly fallen and godless condition, absorbed in a merry meeting with my friends for the morrow or a bit of work that tickles my vanity today, a holiday or a new book, when suddenly a stab of abdominal pain that threatens serious disease, or a headline in the newspapers that threatens us all with destruction, sends this whole pack of cards tumbling down. At first I am overwhelmed, and all my little happinesses look like broken toys. Then, slowly and reluctantly, bit by bit, I try to bring myself into the frame of mind that I should be in at all times. I remind myself that all these toys were never intended to possess my heart, that my true good is in another world, and my only real treasure is Christ. And perhaps, by God's grace, I succeed, and for a day or two become a creature consciously dependent on God and drawing its strength from the right sources. But the moment the threat is withdrawn, my whole nature leaps back to the toys: I am even anxious, God forgive me,

to banish from my mind the only thing that supported me under the threat because it is now associated with the misery of those few days. Thus the terrible necessity of tribulation is only too clear. God has had me for but forty-eight hours and then only by dint of taking everything else away from me. Let Him but sheathe that sword for a moment and I behave like a puppy when the hated bath is over—I shake myself dry as I can and race off to reacquire my comfortable dirtiness, if not in the nearest manure heap, at least in the nearest flower bed. And that is why tribulations cannot cease until God either sees us remade or sees that our remaking is now hopeless.

In our day-to-day lives it is often hard to understand how the tribulations and sufferings we face can be of any value to us. We are often like a little child who can only see the scraped knee and cries out in anguish. One day our three-year-old, Joseph, was running through the house when he tripped and fell against a big potted plant. He hit it with such force that it split open his cheek. Mary, my wife, heard the cry and found Joseph bleeding profusely. Once she was able to get a closer look at the cut, it was clear that it was not going to stop bleeding without four or five stitches. With Joseph tightly pressing a cloth against it, Mary quickly drove him to the local emergency room. When they arrived, the nurse led them into a curtained area and put Joseph up on the exam table. The doctor took one look at his cheek and proceeded to lay out the needle and thread. Despite being three years old, Joseph was always well behaved and usually very stoic during a doctor's visit but this time he couldn't help crying out when the procedure began. Apparently the Novocaine either missed the mark or wasn't working at full strength and he pleaded, "Mom, stop, it hurts. Don't let them do this!" The doctor said it would be over in less than a minute and it was. When Mary related all that had happened, I was reminded of something I had read in *Trust-ful Surrender to Divine Providence: The Secret to Peace and Happiness* by the wonderful missionary, ascetic writer, and spiritual director, St. Claude de la Colombiere, who wrote:

> Imagine the anguish and tears of a mother who is present at a painful operation her child has to undergo. Can anyone doubt on seeing her that she consents to allow the child to suffer only because she expects it to get well and be spared further suffering by means of this violent remedy?
>
> Reason in the same manner when adversity befalls you. You complain that you are ill-treated, insulted, slandered, robbed. Your Redeemer (the name is a tenderer one than that of father or mother), is a witness to all you are suffering. He who loves you and has emphatically declared that whoever touches you touches the apple of His eye, nevertheless allows you to be stricken though He could easily prevent it. Do you hesitate to believe that this passing trial is necessary for the health of your soul?
>
> Even if the Holy Spirit had not called blessed those who suffer, if every page of Scripture did not proclaim aloud the necessity of adversity, if we did not see that suffering is the normal destiny of those who are friends of God, we should still be convinced that it is of untold advantage to us. It is enough to know that the God who chose to suffer all the most horrible tortures the rage of man can invent rather than see us condemned to the slightest pain in the next life is the same God who prepares and offers us the chalice of bitterness we must drink in this world. A God who has so suffered to prevent us from suffering would not make us suffer today to give Himself cruel and pointless pleasure.

This centuries-old wisdom is as applicable today as it was the day it was written. There was Joseph, this little guy, who couldn't comprehend why his mother would allow a stranger to do this painful thing to him. But Mom says, "I know that this is necessary, we've got to stop the bleeding and even though it hurts now, it'll be good for you in the end." Very often in life, God works with us in the same way, and, like Joseph, we're getting the stitches we need for whatever problem we face, while crying out, "Why? Why? Why me?" Meanwhile God is saying to you, "Don't worry, trust me, this passing trial is necessary for the health of your soul. It's going to be okay."

James J. Braddock had to endure his fair share of pain and discomfort too. He was born in the earlier part of the twentieth century in a place affectionately called Hell's Kitchen in New York City. When he was a young boy his parents decided to move across the Hudson River to North Bergen, New Jersey in order to escape the harsh surroundings of the Irish ghetto. He was often found fighting on the streets and was eventually directed to the local boxing club where, by the age of sixteen, he fought his first amateur fight. He was a natural, and by the time he was twenty-one he had won the Golden Gloves light middleweight crown two years in a row.

As a light-heavy weight, he found a way to knock out men twenty or thirty pounds heavier than himself. As a pro he continued his winning ways with twenty-six wins, seventeen by knock-out, and only three losses. His future seemed bright, but in 1930 his career began to unravel with a series of losses and a chronically broken right hand. The result of the stock market crash of 1929 and the impact of the Great Depression were now in full force and, like everyone else, Jimmy and his family were destitute.

One time after breaking his right hand in a fight, a doctor told him that it had not healed properly and it would need to be re-broken and set if he hoped to have full use of it again. With no money to pay for anything, much less the medical procedure, he accepted a fight with the sole purpose of re-breaking his hand so that it could then be set properly. But desperation pushed him to fight again before his hand was fully healed. This time, the break kept him from fighting, and he struggled to provide adequate food, clothing, and shelter for his family. He desperately searched for work of any kind and finally got some hours as a long shore man on the docks in Hoboken.

With his right hand still broken and in a cast he had to do all of the manual labor with his left hand. He did whatever it took to keep the lights on and the babies fed. All day long he would drive hooks into bags of grain or cotton and throw them onto carts with his left hand. When there was no work at the dock he would shovel snow, tend bar, haul garbage, or do whatever else he could find. But the hours were too few and far between to support his young family. Despite his injuries and lack of training and conditioning, he would take any fight he could get just to bring home a few dollars.

Between 1930 and 1933, he lost sixteen times and offers to fight virtually dried up as did the meager purses that accompanied them. He tried moving up to the heavy-weight class but things only seemed to get worse. James J. Braddock was washed-up at the age of twenty-seven.

Having always been self-sufficient, Jimmy was humbled to new depths when desperation drove him to apply for government relief money which would provide his family of five with $6.87 per week or $357.24 annually. Combined with the few extra dollars from whatever work he could find, his family barely survived. Things couldn't have looked more bleak. Yet he never gave up. His undying love for his wife, Mae, and his children fueled his will to take the next step, and the next, and the next.

Finally in 1934 there was a glimmer of hope. A last minute

cancellation sent fight promoters scrambling to find a fighter who had some name recognition but would be an easy opponent for their up-and-coming knock out artist, John "Corn" Griffin. At first they couldn't find anyone willing to take the fight against the number two contender in the world on such short notice. However, James J. Braddock fit the bill nicely and with less than two days before the fight he was offered the bout. For $250 he jumped at the chance even though he hadn't been in the ring since he re-injured his right hand nine months earlier.

As Divine Providence would have it, the Griffin fight was the undercard for the world heavy weight title fight between world champion Primo Carnera and the number one contender, Max Baer. Jimmy's hand had finally healed and to his surprise the work on the docks had made his weaker left hand as strong as his right.

As he entered the ring with Griffin the house was packed with people who had arrived early for the title bout which was to follow. Many of the fans remembered Jimmy but looked on with pity anticipating another humiliating defeat for him. But it was not to be. Three years of hunger and desperation were unleashed on the favorite. After being knocked down by Griffin in the first round, Jimmy came roaring back and dropped Griffin like a sack of potatoes in the third round with a powerful right cross. The fans were stunned and then erupted in jubilation for the under-dog. Afterwards, Jimmy said to his trainer, Joe Gould, "I did that on hash, imagine what I could do with a couple of steaks in me!"

The surprisingly decisive victory did not greatly improve his circumstances. His $150 share of the purse only remained in his hands long enough to pay the delinquent electric and gas bills and to buy milk and a few things for the children to eat. It looked like he was back to where he was before the Griffin fight, desperately in need of money to support his family. The win, however, would prove helpful. Five months later, because of the stir that he caused with his surprise knock-out of Griffin, he was offered the chance to fight a budding superstar by the name of John Henry Lewis.

This was not the first time the two had met. Lewis had badly beaten Jimmy two years earlier in San Francisco and it was thought Braddock would be the ideal pushover for Lewis's New York debut. Lewis had won his last ten fights and was looking to earn a shot at the world title. Braddock, looking aged compared to the vibrant, youthful, Lewis, put on a show. He dropped Lewis in the fifth round and then went on to win the fight by a unanimous decision. The first thing he did with his share of the $750 purse was return to the government relief office and pay back every cent he was given. The little that remained he took home to Mae who carefully managed it to go as far as possible. Although she wished he didn't box, she was grateful.

Four months after the Lewis fight Jimmy was back in the ring again, this time going against Art Lasky, one of the top challengers for the heavy weight title. Lasky was a mountain of a man at 6'4" and weighed fifteen pounds more than Jimmy. Despite the previous two upsets, Jimmy was still seen as a washed-up, ten-to-one, underdog. Lasky needed one more good fight to secure a title match with Max Baer, the reigning world champion, and he thought Jimmy would be a popular and easy road to the championship fight. In the first round Jimmy came out and broke Lasky's nose. Despite several rounds of brutal head and body shots by Lasky, Jimmy weathered the storm and won in a fifteen round unanimous decision.

If this wasn't miraculous enough, two of the other major contenders for the world crown were eliminated from contention during the same period. Max Schmeling, the German fighter, was the number one challenger that everyone in the boxing world wanted to see in a rematch against Max Baer for the title. Once again, Providence intervened and plans fell through,

leaving Baer looking for a title defense match until the Schmeling match could be arranged. At this point James J. Braddock
was the next legitimate challenger in line and the championship fight was scheduled with Max Baer for June 13, 1935. Upon
learning that the contract had been signed, Baer said, "They just
signed the poor guy's death warrant."

Baer not only outweighed Jimmy by fifteen or twenty pounds
but had also won the crown by destroying the former 6'6" 265 lb.
world champion, Primo Carnera. Baer's right hand punch was
so devastating that he actually killed Frankie Campbell during a
bout on August 25, 1930. Two years later Baer knocked out the
6'3" 215 pound Ernie Shaff who had received such a tremendous
beating before going down that he died from a brain aneurysm
several months after their fight. No one believed that Jimmy had
the slightest chance of defeating Max Baer. In fact, many people
strongly believed that he would not leave the ring alive.

Braddock's downward spiral may have begun with his loss
to light-heavy weight champion, Tommy Loughran, but now
it seemed that Loughran would be his answer to fighting Baer.
Jimmy had studied Loughran's style and realized that he didn't
try to go for the big knockout punch against a stronger opponent. Instead he would keep moving by constantly circling
and jabbing away from the other fighters dominant punch and
then look for an opportunity to get in close. This is how Jimmy
decided to fight Baer who was taking the fight lightly believing that Braddock was an old man clinging to a career that was
long over.

What Baer didn't realize is that Braddock had been forged
in the fire of adversity and suffering for the past five years. It
made him tougher and stronger than he had ever been and it
also made him a favorite among the people. They saw him as an
ordinary guy who had suffered through the Great Depression
just like they did, where one out of every three people stood on

a soup line daily. He wasn't built like some freak of nature, he looked like them too. He was an average man, who never gave up, loved his wife and children, and gave people hope in a better tomorrow.

On the night Jimmy entered the ring with Max Baer all he could see was the hovel that Mae, the children, and he had lived in for the past five years. He said, "Whether it goes one round or three rounds or ten rounds, it will be a fight and a fight all the way. When you've been through what I've had to face in the last two years, a Max Baer or a Bengal tiger looks like a house pet. He might come at me with a cannon and a blackjack and he would still be a picnic compared to what I've had to face." It was clear that Max Baer would have to kill him before he would lose this fight.

Baer weighed eighteen pounds more than his challenger, was four years younger, and had a three inch reach advantage. As much as the crowd was behind Jimmy the betting money was on Baer. The fight began with Baer clowning around, striking poses, and waving to popular figures in the front rows. Jimmy was all business and won the first three rounds on points. In the fourth, Baer staggered Jimmy as the bell ended and won the round. Baer fouled Jimmy in the fifth but he would have lost the round based on performance anyway. The sixth and seventh were Baer's. He won the seventh round by momentarily wobbling Jimmy with a short powerful right hand punch to his jaw.

By now the entire crowd was in Jimmy's corner. Their support only grew as Baer clowned around in the eighth and feigned being hurt by a missed right cross. Baer lost the ninth round for a low blow. Realizing that he was now in serious trouble and that the fight was slipping away from him, Baer unleashed a torrent of punches and easily won the tenth and eleventh rounds. He probably would have won the twelfth except for another foul that cost him the round. Jimmy came back strong in the thirteenth as the crowd was on their feet chanting "Braddock! Braddock! Braddock!" In desperation, Baer gave it all he had in the final two rounds but he could do nothing against the Loughran strategy that Jimmy used to perfection.

As the fight ended the crowd erupted again chanting Jimmy's name. Everyone knew he had done what was thought impossible; he had won. The ring announcer said, "The winner and new . . ." the rest of it was drowned out by the deafening cheer of the crowd. He had done the impossible.

On January 21, 1938, after winning a fight with Tommy Farr, Jimmy said, "This is my farewell to boxing, a sport which owes me nothing, and to which I owe everything—the many friends I have made, and the means with which I have been able to provide for my family." He went on to serve as a Lieutenant in the army during World War II followed by many years of hard work on the same docks that had helped make him a champion. At the age of sixty-nine, he died peacefully in his sleep. He and Mae had spent forty-four years of marriage loving each other and raising their children in the same home they had bought almost forty years earlier. By all accounts, James J. Braddock was a good and virtuous man all of his life. Red Smith, one of America's most popular sportswriters at the time wrote, "If death came easily, it was the only thing in his life that did."

Considering the life and times of James J. Braddock might lead you to ask, "Why were my grandparents and their parents so tough? How were they able to survive such harsh lives, sometimes working two or three jobs? How did they take the pain and fatigue? And why do I seem to tire so easily?" Part of the answer can be found in the conveniences and luxuries of today. It wasn't so long ago that most people spent their entire lives working for the basic necessities of life. Their days were spent in hard labor to provide enough food, clothing and shelter to keep their families safe and sound. The brief evenings before bed were filled with good conversation among family and friends. Few of them ever traveled beyond the place of their births and news from other parts of the country spread slowly from town to town.

Today we wonder what people did before there were channel changers. It's hard to imagine that they actually got up and walked over to the television to change the channel manually. The more we sit around the more our muscles literally waste away, and often our minds along with them.

It won't take long to see the inevitable muscular atrophy that comes from disuse. Soon you will need your own lift chair to help you sit and stand. Once the Lift-o-matic launches you onto your feet, you can shuffle outside to get some real work done while reclining on your rolling garden seat. In stark contrast, I can still see my eighty-six-year old, Irish born grandfather wearing his bibbed-overalls on a hot summer day while swinging a pick axe as he dug up a rocky patch of soil for his tomato garden in my parents' backyard. Not everyone comes from such a poor and humble beginning or is born with such good health and longevity, but certainly our growing dependence on conveniences only speeds up the process of becoming feeble and dependent.

Are you allowing trains, planes, and automobiles, paper plates and cups, microwaves, supermarkets, chainsaws, riding mowers, washers, dryers, wrinkle free clothes, elevators, escalators, moving walkways, and shopping online, to name only a few, to soften you up? With every push of a button and every joule of energy saved we are one step closer to becoming the bedridden grandparents in *Willy Wonka and the Chocolate Factory.* Like Grandpa Joe we need to venture out from under the covers and learn to walk again. The less physical, mental and spiritual pain and discomfort we experience in our daily lives, the less we will be able to take it when it comes. And it always comes.

Children are not immune from this pain and discomfort. As a matter of fact they are more vulnerable to it because they have fewer resources than an adult and they will experience the adverse side effects of a softer life earlier than their harder working grandparents did. Children are atrophying before our eyes. They are losing muscle and gaining fat at a terrifying rate. They are becoming more self absorbed and slothful. They are not taught to be long suffering or to tolerate discomfort of any kind. It begins with little things like the philosophy that everyone gets a trophy, which builds neither virtue, nor the ability to suffer, nor the ability to be a gracious loser. Children are led to believe that everyone deserves a prize regardless of effort or performance.

Even the NFL has begun a program called Play60. Can you believe that we are at the point where we have to try to cajole children into being active for an hour a day! Limiting children's TV and computer time would go a long way to reducing the number of couch potatoes. Children, not text messages, should be flying around the ball fields and playgrounds!

As much as we shy away from physical pain and discomfort, sometimes it is the easiest kind to endure. In the *Great Divorce*, C.S. Lewis wrote about letting go of spiritual and mental attachments that prevent us from being truly happy, eternally happy. We are able to see ourselves in the characters Lewis describes and we can imagine our own struggle to be free from the things that oppress us and prevent us from being happy. He provides us with an insight into the painful, and yet rewarding, process of letting go and allowing grace to transform us. The story begins with a man at a bus stop in what appears to be a small town in England. However, instead of a trip across town, he is shortly confronted with a choice about where he will spend eternity. When the bus finally reaches its destination somewhere between Heaven and hell, he observes other souls as they are confronted with the painful task of extinguishing their selfish desires. In this excerpt, one of these souls, or ghosts as Lewis describes them, is challenged to find a purpose sufficient to overcome the pain that he must undergo.

He is approached by a being who is radiating the most intense light and heat. On the shoulder of the ghost sits a red lizard with a whip-like tail who is continually whispering destructive advice into the ear of the ghost. As the ghost attempts to leave he is asked by the angel why he is leaving so soon. The ghost explains that the lizard is causing too many problems and that he needs to take him back home.

> "Would you like me to make him quiet?" said the flaming Spirit-an angel, as I now understood.
>
> "Of course I would," said the Ghost.
>
> "Then I will kill him," said the Angel, taking a step forward.
>
> "Oh-ah-look out! You're burning me. Keep away," said the Ghost, retreating.
>
> "Don't you want him killed?"

Each time the ghost is asked by the angel, "May I kill it?" the ghost finds one rationalization after another to avoid what he perceives to be a painful operation. The angel informs him there is only one way to rid him of the lizard and that is to kill it. The ghost assures the angel that he will come back another day when he is feeling better.

> "There is no other day. All days are present now."
>
> "Get back! You're burning me. How can I tell you to kill it? You'd kill me if you did."
>
> "It is not so."
>
> "Why, you're hurting me now."
>
> "I never said it wouldn't hurt you. I said it wouldn't kill you."
>
> "Oh, I know. You think I'm a coward. But it isn't

that. Really it isn't. I say! Let me run back by tonight's bus and get an opinion from my own doctor. I'll come again the first moment I can."

"This moment contains all moments."

"Why are you torturing me? You are jeering at me. How can I let you tear me to pieces? If you wanted to help me, why didn't you kill the damned thing without asking me–before I knew? It would be all over by now if you had."

"I cannot kill it against your will. It is impossible. Have I your permission?"

Here the lizard increases his efforts to convince the ghost that he should leave immediately and have nothing more to do with this terrible thing.

"Have I your permission?" said the Angel to the Ghost.

"I know it will kill me."

"It won't. But supposing it did?"

"You're right. It would be better to be dead than to live with this creature."

"Then I may?"

"Damn and blast you! Go on can't you? Get it over. Do what you like," bellowed the Ghost: but ended, whimpering, "God help me. God help me."

The ghost finally assents and the angel quickly steps forward and in an instant crushes the lizard and throws it to the ground. Moments later the ghost is transformed into a being of light.

The painful operation of removing the lizard of vice from our shoulders can seem overwhelming and beyond our capacity, but we have a choice. We can either remain mired in endless purposeless pain or we can give our consent to begin a life-changing transformation; to become new and as bright as the sun; to finally possess the strength to leap upon the great stallion's back and race across the brilliant fields of green to our heavenly home.

This requires a strong purpose and the courage to exercise our wills to change. General Patton once said, "Fatigue makes cowards of us all. Men in condition do not tire." This means that overcoming pain and fatigue requires some action on our part. It will require training and preparation to endure and not to give up. "But that is for brave men and women and I am not brave," you might be tempted to say. Patton has a response, "If we take the generally accepted definition of bravery as a quality which knows not fear, I have never seen a brave man. All men are frightened. The more intelligent they are, the more they are frightened. The courageous man is the man who forces himself, in spite of his fear, to carry on. . . . Courage is fear holding out a minute longer." (General George S. Patton, Jr., *War As I Knew It*, 1947). Another way of describing "the man who forces himself" is "the man who wills himself" to do what is right in spite of any criticism or adversity, including fear.

Practicing virtue in small ways strengthens and conditions your will to respond well when you are faced with real crises in your life. A story in the old Boy Scout book, *The Practice of the Oath and Law*, describes two brothers who go to war together. One of the brothers is severely wounded during a battle and the other, upon returning from the field, learns that his younger brother did not make it back to camp and is still laying somewhere out on the battlefield. He asks permission of his commanding officer to go out and bring his younger brother back but his request is denied. "The officer tells him, 'Your brother is probably dead and there is no point in you risking your life to bring in his body.' But the older brother is relentless and continues his pleading until the officer finally consents. Just as the older brother finally reaches the camp, carrying his severely wounded brother across his shoulders, the younger brother dies. 'There, you see,' said the officer, 'You risked your life for nothing.' 'No,' replied Tom, 'I did what he expected of me and I have my reward. When I crept up to him and took him in my arms, he said, 'Tom, I knew you would come.'"

There is a touching song that parallels the story of Tom and his brother, written by Edward Madden, called "Two Little Boys." The best recording of the tune was performed as a 90th Anniversary Tribute to the ending of World War I by Rolf Harris and the Froncysyllte Male Voice Choir. The use of trumpets and the powerful men's voices conveys the camaraderie, loyalty and brotherhood found among soldiers in every war. It was composed sometime after the end of the American Civil War and recounts the unbreakable bond of friendship and love that two little boys share all of their lives. The song captures the essence of Tom's willingness to sacrifice his life for his brother in a way that words alone might not be able to convey.

> TWO LITTLE BOYS
> (Original Lyrics)
>
> Two little boys
> Had two little toys,
> Each was a wooden horse;
> Gaily they'd play
> Each summer's day—
> Warriors both of course.
> One little chap
> Then had a mishap,
> Broke off his horse's head;
> Wept for his toy,
> Then cried with joy
> As his young comrade said:

"Did you think I would leave you crying
When there's room on my horse for you?
Climb up here, Joe, and don't be sighing;
He can go just as fast with two.
When we grow up we'll both be soldiers,
And our horses will not be toys;
Then I wonder if you'll remember
When we were two little boys."

Long years passed,
The war came at last;
Gaily they marched away.
Cannon roar'd loud
Midst the mad crowd
Wounded and dying Jack lay.
Loud rings a cry—
A horse dashes by,
From out the ranks of blue,
Gallops away
To where Jack lay
As a voice comes strong and true:

"Did you think I would leave you dying
When there's room on my horse for you?
Climb up here Jack, we'll soon be flying
To the ranks of the boys in blue.
Did you say, Jack, I'm all a-tremble,
Well perhaps it's the battle's noise;
Or it may be that I remember
When we were two little boys."

"There you have the gist of it all; somebody expects something fine and noble and unselfish of us; someone expects us to be faithful." (*The Practice of the Oath and Law*) Who in your life expects you to be faithful and virtuous? Is your purpose clear and strong? Can you take the pain and discomfort required of you? Don't stop to count the cost or to ask whether the sacrifice required to do the right thing is worth doing. It is, and it always will be. A life of virtue will prepare you to ask, "Did you think I would leave you dying?" And those who know you well, will melt your heart with their confident reply, "I knew you would come."

In your search for a purpose strong enough to endure all suffering, the Act of Contrition has an insight that may be helpful to you. It is a prayer asking for God's forgiveness for the things you have done wrong and the things that you have failed to do. In it you say, "O my God, I am heartily sorry for having offended Thee and I detest all my sins because of Thy just punishment; but most of all because I have offended Thee my God who are all good and deserving of all of my love. I firmly resolve, with the help of thy grace, to sin no more and to avoid the near occasion of sin." It is a simple and beautiful prayer. Note that there are two reasons for being sorry. The first is the lower argument: you fear God's just punishment, the pains of hell. The second is the higher argument: you are truly sorry because God is deserving of all your love; you want to do the right thing no matter how difficult it may be because you love Him. Ask yourself, "Is fear of discomfort my primary motivation, my purpose, or is it something higher?"

If properly directed, sport provides the perfect environment for cultivating and strengthening our ability to sacrifice and live virtuous lives. *Brian's Song*, the true life story about the relationship and personal struggles of Chicago Bears' running backs Gayle Sayers and Brian Piccolo, reveals the way sport can transform boys into men of virtue. The problems that we attribute to sport are not about sport. Sport provides an artificial environment that is neither good nor bad. In reality it is the athletes, coaches, referees, organizers, parents, and fans who participate in it that make it one way or the other.

TAKE AWAY

Pain without a purpose is intolerable to human beings. The greater the purpose, the greater the sacrifice you will be able to make and the more readily you will be able to accept the tribulations that come your way. Preparing yourself mentally, physically and spiritually through each grace-filled and virtuous act of your life is the only way to become strong enough to endure and accept the pain and sacrifice that is asked of you each day. Consider the lesson of "Two Little Boys." Practicing virtue in the nursery led to generosity, loyalty, friendship, love, courage and joy on the battlefield, when lives hung in the balance. What is your ultimate purpose? The stronger it is, the more pain and discomfort you can take, the greater your ability and desire to sacrifice. And ultimately the happier you'll be.

CHAPTER 10

LESS THAN A MINUTE TO GO

TIME. It is the only thing that we can't get back. There never seems to be enough of it. We are always looking for more of it. Maybe that's why the last few seconds of a close game are so riveting. Everything seems to be on the line and we are not sure how it is going to end.

What if you were just told that you only had ten minutes to live? Would life be different for you? What would you do? Who would you talk to? As with Scrooge, in Charles Dickens' *A Christmas Carol*, your life would seem to flash before your eyes. Certainly your life, with the few minutes that remained, would be different than it is now. If so, an important question to ask would be, "How do I know that I will not die in the next ten minutes?" The answer is pretty obvious: You don't know. If you agree that your life would be different if you were going to die in the next few minutes, why are you not living that way right now? It is because you don't believe that you will die in the next ten minutes and therefore there is no need to change now. Given the eternal consequences, that's a pretty big gamble.

Blaise Pascal, a seventeenth-century mathematician, took this idea a little further when he posited what has come to be known as "Pascal's Wager." He challenges those individuals who are living without any conviction or belief to consider their end. The Wager is not a proof for the existence of God, but it is a clever way of getting people who had no belief to reconsider their position.

The Wager begins by showing that you have been born and there is no way to stop the process of aging and dying. Therefore, to believe or not to believe is like making a wager. You might ask, "What if I choose not to place a bet?" Too late, the clock is running. Your life is finite; it is going to end at some point. You are placing a bet whether you know it or not. Your action or lack thereof will determine which one you made. Paschal described the four possible outcomes and then challenged his readers to decide which one they should place their bet on. The first possibility was to wager for the existence of God and then at the end of your life discover that he does indeed exist. This would result in your infinite happiness. The second possibility was to wager for the existence of God but then in the end discover that he does not exist. Nothing lost by having lived a good life. The third possibility was to wager against the existence of God and then in the end discover that he really does exist. This results in the worst possible outcome, infinite loss. The fourth and final possibility was to wager against the existence of God and then discover at the end of your life that he did not exist. Nothing gained. Since the first wager is the best one to make because it leads to infinite happiness, Paschal concludes that his readers should begin considering who is God and what is their relationship with Him.

Whether you live ten or ten million minutes more, your entire happiness in life depends on love. Why? The simple answer is, "Because God made you that way." If you are happy it is because you love someone and they love you. Nothing will ever be more important to you in life. Sure we all get distracted or sometimes think the pursuit of money, power, fame or pleasure is most important but in the end we all know the truth. St.

Augustine captured it in these beautiful words, "Our hearts are restless until they rest in You." Our strongest purpose in life is love. And God is love.

Consider the basis of any person's relationship. If you are a young man, imagine having just turned twenty-one years of age and a group of your friends invite you to a special birthday dinner at your favorite restaurant. During the course of the evening you begin speaking with Dave, a friend of a friend you have just met for the first time. He begins to tell you about this woman, Rebecca MacIntyre, who he met while on a trip in Alaska. At first you are not interested in hearing about Alaska or Rebecca the tour guide, but he goes on for what seems like an hour raving about her beauty, intelligence and soul. Your interest is piqued but you eventually drift back into conversation with your friends until the wonderful evening comes to an end.

On your way home you begin to think about Rebecca in Alaska. When you arrive back in your apartment, a strange thought pops into your head, "I wonder if she can be as good as Dave described?" An even stranger urge comes over you to call her. You begin calling information and finally come across a phone number that might just be hers. You take a deep breath and begin dialing the number. After three or four rings, a lovely voice answers, "Hello." You fumble around for a moment before explaining, "You see, it is my Birthday and . . . I met Dave . . . who told me all about you and his tour of Alaska and . . . I just had to call because you sounded too good to be true." There is silence on the other end of the line until finally she says, "Well, happy birthday!"

The two of you begin talking and before you know it three hours have passed. Rebecca and you have connected in a way that had never happened for either of you. Almost as one, you both excitedly agree to meet in Calgary, half way between New York and Anchorage. When you finally meet face-to-face it surpasses all expectations. By the end of the week, you both decide that you want to spend more time together. It turns out Rebecca has a cousin in New York that she can stay with and the Cruise line she works for has an office downtown.

When Rebecca arrives in New York, you pick her up at the airport and begin driving her to where she will be staying with her cousin. When Rebecca tells you the address you sit there dumbfounded. The address is four houses down from where you grew up. It turns out that it is the house Rebecca lived in before her family moved to Anchorage. She even went to the same school that you did! Weeks and months go by with dates and calls and before long there is a wedding. Year after year, your love for each other grows ever deeper with each selfless act and shared experience. Rebecca is no longer a name in Alaska. Rebecca has become someone you would die for.

Your relationship with God is much the same. Some people say, "I don't think much about God. I just don't have any emotion or strong feeling about Him." Rebecca was just a name in Alaska until you met her, dated her, married her, and continued to sacrifice for her. All of that led you to think about her all the time and built a strong love and emotional tie with her. The question to ask yourself is, "Is God a name in Alaska or someone I would die for?" It may be the former now, but if you are willing to take the chance and make the first call it might not be too long before it's the latter.

The good news is that we don't have to do it all on our own. God provides the grace and all we are asked to do is cooperate with it. The bad news is that sometimes we forget that and try to muscle our way through the situation or task. It is the difference between trying to lift weights on your own or having someone to spot you when you begin to fail, and having an expert strength and conditioning coach who designs a program especially for you and is there to help when the bar gets a little too heavy.

You may have experienced some tough and difficult times in your life and felt like you were abandoned, when in fact the grace was pouring down like Niagara Falls. You were standing under it with your umbrella up complaining that there was no grace for you and wondering why you weren't getting wet. If you could have listened more closely you would have heard someone shouting, "Put down the umbrella!" Unlike Niagara Falls the grace available to us is infinite. We could be permanently wet with it if we would only stay focused. The umbrellas that we all have up are the things that distract us from what we were made to be, which is happy.

With that grace raining down, have you ever been so overwhelmed by gratitude that you didn't know what to say or do because nothing seemed adequate to express your thankfulness? That is what happens when you put down your umbrella and let the grace pour down on you.

Take a minute or two and write down on a piece of paper all of the things in your life that are invaluable, meaning beyond worth. You wouldn't trade them for all the money in the world. After about a minute most people have stopped writing. Let's review your list. For example did you write down your brain stem? Or how about your left and right retinas? Or each of the nuclei contained in every cell of your body? Initially you probably had a look on your face that said, "What is he talking about?" But think about it. Can you live with cells that have no nucleus? No! Now reconsider your list. You probably wrote down big things like, my health, my family, and so on, without considering all of the invaluable things that make up each one. To make a proper list you would need an almost infinite number of pads and pencils to write down all of the things that could not be bought with all of the world's treasure.

We are wealthy beyond understanding. If we had everything taken away from us today and we lived another hundred years, we could never sufficiently thank God for all that he has given us to this point in time. It is mortifying to consider how often we complain about this discomfort or that inconvenience in our daily lives when we have so much to be thankful for. With umbrellas down, let us be overwhelmed with gratitude by recognizing the infinite blessings in our lives.

Consider Irish 1500 meters runner Ron Delaney who prior to the start of his Olympic race said, "I resigned myself quietly to the will of God and prayed not so much for victory but for the grace to run up to my capabilities." After winning the 1500 meters Gold Medal at the 1956 Melbourne Olympic Games, Delaney knelt down in prayer of thanksgiving because, "I had to say, 'Thank you,' to God for the gift I was given." It is worth noting that John Landy, legendary miler and man of virtue who lost to Delaney, came to his aid not realizing he was praying.

However, in recent years there seems to be less tolerance for athletes who publicly discuss their belief in God or engage in public displays of devotion. Tim Tebow rocked the NFL with his dramatic, unorthodox come-from-behind wins to lead the Denver Broncos to the playoffs but he was continually criticized for displaying signs of his faith on the sidelines or after a game. Commentators were leery of him, believing he must have some ulterior motive. No one in the NFL could actually be trying to live a good and moral life, right?

In the 2008 Beijing Olympics the Chinese government tried to discourage displays of faith by citing the recently modified Olympic Charter to prohibit "political, religious or racial propaganda." Clearly this is not what the founder of the modern Olympic Games, Baron Pierre de Coubertin, believed the Games were meant to do. During a 1935 radio broadcast on the sixtieth anniversary of the Games he said:

The first essential characteristic of the Modern Olympics is that, like the Olympics of ancient Greece, they constitute a religion . . . It is in this principle that all the religious observances which go to make up the ceremonial of the Modern Games have their origin. I have had to fight to render these observances acceptable to the world one by one, public opinion remaining for a considerable time antagonistic towards them, while seeing in them mere theatrical shows, purposeless spectacles quite out of keeping with the solemn dignity of international sporting competitions. The idea of the interdependence of religion and sport, this 'religio athletae', has taken a long time to achieve assimilation into the minds of the competitors and there are still many of them who do not put it into practice, except unconsciously; but they will gradually come round to it.

He would be happy to know that many athletes are living the example that he hoped they would. When asked about her genuflection and prayer of gratitude after an Olympic race, Sanya Richards said: "It's important because I want people to know that I'm not the best because I'm Sanya Richards. I'm the best because of God. I truly believe we can't will ourselves to win. I hope people see the same thing I see." Perhaps more importantly, she expresses the same faith when facing difficult times. After a particularly disappointing finish in the Beijing Olympic Games she said, "I've learned that God is always on time! Sometimes things happen that we can't understand, and we think that God has forgotten about us, but that is never true. We must go through different seasons to truly appreciate how God is working everything out for us. In the meantime, we must thank God in all things!"

Perhaps this reality is captured best in the greatest sports quote of all time which came from the most unlikely source imaginable, Pope Pius XII, speaking in an address to a group of male soccer coaches entitled "Sport at the Service of the Spirit":

> Sport, properly directed, develops character, makes a man courageous, a generous loser, and a gracious victor; it refines the senses, gives intellectual penetration, and steels the will to endurance. It is not merely a physical development then. Sport, rightly understood, is an occupation of the whole man, and while perfecting the body as an instrument of the mind, it also makes the mind itself a more refined instrument for the search and communication of truth and helps man to achieve that end to which all others must be subservient, the service and praise of his Creator.

For those who still believe we should banish all forms of faith from the playing fields, consider the wisdom of the Duke of Sutherland's remarks concerning Eric Liddle who refused to run on Sunday at the 1924 Paris Olympic Games. "The 'lad' as you call him is a true man of principles and a true athlete. His speed is a mere extension of his life, its force. We sought to sever his running from himself." Have we come to believe that you can sever one from the other? R. Emmett Tyrrel, founder and editor-in-chief of the American Spectator, summed it up nicely when he wrote, "Thanking God for victory after an event, or asking for his help before an event, is not 'propaganda' as mentioned in the revised Olympic charter. It is prayer. Where prayer is viewed unfavorably no civilized person should want to be."

On the other hand, if an athlete attributes his success to his lucky socks that he hasn't washed in six years or an entire team turns their baseball caps inside out and upside down, it is considered cool, even worthy of imitation. If people come to a game in sub-freezing temperatures with their half naked bodies painted in team colors, they are seen as loyal and true fans. But if a player kneels down or blesses himself he is either a con artist or a religious fanatic.

We all want to believe in something beyond ourselves but it seems that we tend to fill the void with something less than the real thing or with some kind of counterfeit. Maybe it is more comfortable for some people to discuss and participate in rituals and superstitions than to think about God and their ultimate purpose in life. It somehow seems easier or less personal to attach our hopes to "lucky" objects or behaviors.

Interestingly, the criticism about religion being a crutch seems odd since players come to completely depend on some fabricated ritual or object to help them perform well. The player who has to touch his leg, then his elbow, then his helmet, tap the plate, dig his shoes into the dirt exactly four times, in sequence, before every pitch, in order to hit well has made up his own religion.

The reason he does this is to try to ease the pressure that he is feeling to perform well. Instead of controlling the situation, he abdicates his responsibility and hands over his destiny to the object or the ritual. If he strikes out the first thing he does is to check to make sure that he is actually wearing his lucky socks. If he is, then he has to figure out why they didn't work! If he gets a hit he says, "I knew it, these socks are golden. They can't miss!" If he does well he is lucky. If something bad happens, "Why did God let that happen?" We should at least be fair and attribute either both to luck or to God.

The phrase "life is stranger than fiction," is really an acknowledgement that Divine Providence is always at work and, more often than not, beyond our ability to predict or understand it. A couple of years ago I met Rich Donnelly when we were inducted into the Sports Faith International Hall of Fame and heard a remarkable story about his daughter Amy.

Rich's life is a story of the prodigal son's return. From 1985 to 1996 he was the third base coach for the Pittsburgh Pirates.

In 1992 after a spring training workout in Bradenton, FL, Rich was sitting on the floor of his apartment when he received a call from his daughter Amy. With eight children this didn't seem unusual because he was getting calls from them all the time. She said, "Hi Dad, I have something to tell you." He thought, "At seventeen years of age this could be anything." She said, "Dad . . . I have a brain tumor . . . and I am sorry." He sat there momentarily stunned by the devastating news. Then he said, "What do you have to be sorry for?" But that was Amy, more concerned about her Dad, and always thinking about others first. A week later she had surgery. When the operation was over the surgeon came out and told Rich and his wife that they were not able to get all of the tumor and that she only had about nine months to live.

They were crushed by the news but resolved to fight it. Amy immediately began the long and debilitating treatment at Children's Hospital in Dallas. Rich continued working to support the family and provide for Amy's needs and the rest of the family did all they could to be there for her. The Pirates were scheduled to play the Atlanta Braves for the National League pennant. Rich had a dear friend in Dallas who offered to fly Amy up to see the fifth game of the series. The chemotherapy was taking its toll on Amy. She had lost all of her hair and she was feeling very weak but she never showed it. She was just happy to be there with her Dad and away from the hospital for a couple of days. Rich was so happy that Amy was there and winning the game was like icing on the cake.

She and her Dad were driving home after the game, when Amy, who was in the back seat, leaned forward and asked, "Dad, when you have a man on second base and you get in that stance of yours, in the third base coaching box, and cup your hands around your mouth and yell out to him, what are you telling those guys, 'The chicken runs at midnight' or what?" Rich said,

"What? Where the heck did you get that one?" Amy laughed, "I don't know it just came out."

The next day Amy headed back to Texas to continue her treatment. When Rich arrived in the dugout for the seventh game of the National League Championship Series, someone handed him a message that had come into the club house. It simply read, "The chicken runs at midnight. Love Amy." While he was still staring at it and smiling, Pirates second baseman Jose Lind, who spoke very little English, came over to ask, "What's that?" Rich, half talking and laughing to himself, said, "The chicken runs at midnight." Moments later, as Jose ran onto the field to start the game he yelled out for everyone to hear, "Okay, let's go! The chicken runs at midnight!" Even though no one knew what it meant, it sounded funny and everyone on the team seemed to adopt it. Going into the ninth inning the Pirates were winning 2-0. Rich had told Amy before she left, "If we make it to the World Series, you are coming!" With one out to go, the Braves rallied from behind and ended up winning the game on an RBI single by Francisco Cabrera. Rich's season was over. No World Series for Amy.

The next three months went all too fast for Rich and his family. Amy's condition had gradually worsened and in early January, she slipped into a coma and never regained consciousness. On January 23, 1993 Amy passed away. Shortly after the funeral, the Donnellys all went to the cemetery to pick out the marker for Amy's grave. Rich said, "The people at the cemetery wanted to put all of these flowery phrases on her tombstone. We said, 'No, no, no! We are going to change things up. We want you to put *The chicken runs at midnight* on her gravestone.'"

It was extraordinarily difficult to cope with Amy's death but the Donnellys did their best to go on. Rich continued as the third base coach with the Pirates for two more seasons before moving on to the Florida Marlins with team manager Jim Leyland. The Marlins had only been in existence since 1992, but by 1997 they found themselves in the playoffs against the Atlanta Braves. This time, Rich was on the winning side as the Marlins won the series 4-2.

The 1997 World Series was one of the most exciting ever played. The Marlins won the first game of the best-of-seven series. The Cleveland Indians battled back and took the second game. Back and forth they went, trading wins until they arrived at the decisive seventh game. The Indians had a big third inning to take a 2-0 lead. In the seventh inning, Marlins outfielder Bobby Bonilla sent one into the stands to make it 2-1. Cleveland's star closer, Jose Mesa, was sent to the mound in the bottom of the ninth to close out the series. Moises Alou led off for the Marlins with a single to center field. Bonilla then struck out swinging for the first out. Catcher Charlie Johnson singled and moved Alou to third base. With men on first and third, Craig Counsell came to the plate and hit a towering shot that drove right fielder Manny Ramirez back to the warning track for the second out. But it was deep enough to bring Alou home and tie the game at 2-2.

Into extra innings they went but neither team could score in the tenth. In the bottom of the eleventh with the score still tied the Marlins came to bat. Bonilla led off with a single. Greg Zaun attempted to bunt him over to second, but popped it up to pitcher Charles Nagy for the first out. Counsell followed with what should have been an inning ending double play but second baseman Tony Fernandez misplayed the routine ground ball allowing Counsell to reach first and Bonilla to advance to third. With one out, the Indians decided to intentionally walk the next batter. With bases loaded, Devon White hit a ground ball and Bonilla was retired at home plate on a fielder's choice for the second out. Shortstop Edgar Renteria then came to the plate and hit a high bouncing ground ball right towards the pitcher. Nagy threw up his glove and grazed the ball, but was unable to stop it from sailing into center field. A hit! Counsell ran home and the Marlins had won the World Series!

Seventh game of the World Series, tie score, bottom of the eleventh inning, two outs, and Rich Donnelly waves home Craig Counsell from third base to win the game. Counsell, also known as the "Chicken," had been given the nickname by Rich's son Tim Donnelly because he flapped his left elbow like a chicken before every pitch. When Counsell leaped into the air and landed on home plate, the euphoric fans and players went wild. Everyone was jumping up and down and yelling. Rich said, "I was running around grabbing people, kissing and hugging people, I didn't know who's who. All of a sudden I see my son, Tim and he's running at me. Something is wrong. He's crying. He's screaming. Something's wrong. I'm thinking he should be happy but he's screaming and crying. I shout above the roar, 'What's wrong?' He says, 'Dad, look!' 'Look where,' I say? He says, 'Look behind you!' I look around to see the stadium clock; it's twelve o'clock! Tim said, 'Dad, the chicken runs at midnight! The chicken runs at midnight!' I went from complete joy to feeling like all the air had just been sucked out of my body." The "Chicken," Craig Counsell, had scored the winning run at midnight, just as Amy had said four years earlier. As Rich's voices cracks, he says, "Amy knew how much it would mean to me to win a World Series. She had to be there with me; I have no doubt in my mind that she was."

Amy's death and her prophetic line, the chicken runs at midnight, forever changed Rich Donnelly. He had drifted away from God and had become self absorbed. He said, "Amy taught me that here are two kinds of people in the world, those who are humble, and those who are about to be. In my life, it was 'about to be.' My ego had gotten out of hand and it's a shame that it took her death to bring me down to where I could say, 'Hey, you ain't what you think you are. It's not about you. It's about everyone else. It's about doing the right thing." Somehow God brought good out of suffering. Rich's faith has been renewed and strengthened and he found that Amy's story has helped so many parents cope with the loss of their child. Amy, who wanted to be a teacher and lived everyday like it was her birthday, is still teaching and still giving.

After the celebration ended, Rich and his two sons, Tim and Mike, sat in the car thinking about Amy and wishing they could call her. Rich pulled out the note that he always carried in his pocket which read, "Dear Dad, The chicken runs at midnight, Love Amy." They sat there a little longer wishing the moment of celebration with her would never end but it never really would. Rich still carries Amy's note in his pocket to this day. She is with him night and day reminding him that there are no accidents, only Divine Providence.

There may be no one who knew that better than Job. In *Trustful Surrender to Divine Providence*, Father Jean Baptiste Saint Jure, S.J., wrote,

> We have a celebrated example [of absolute faith and trust] in Job. He loses his children and his possessions; he falls from the height of fortune to the depths of poverty. And he says, "The Lord gave and the Lord hath taken away. As it hath pleased the Lord, so is it done. Blessed be the name of the Lord." "Note," observes St. Augustine, "Job does not say, 'The Lord gave and the devil hath taken away' but says, wise that he is, 'The Lord gave me my children and my possessions, and it is He who has taken them away; it has been done as it pleased the Lord.'"

You may find it comforting to know that if you are struggling or suffering greatly, you are not alone. Like Job, there are countless men and women who accepted God's will in all things and chose to use their suffering for the good of others.

Walter J. Ciszek, S.J. was just such a man. He endured more than twenty years of torture and hard labor in Soviet prisons and Siberian labor camps and survived to write about them in two books, *He Leadeth Me* and *With God in Russia*. These are must reads if you want to understand how someone can cope with physical, mental and spiritual pain while living through numerous near death experiences and still come out loving people.

Rick Strom a ten year NFL veteran and former back-up quarterback for the Pittsburgh Steelers said, "I read *He Leadeth Me* before every preseason training camp. I thought, 'My God, if Walter Ciszek could shovel coal for twelve hours a day while living on bread crusts and still find God's will, then certainly as a well paid professional athlete, I could go out on a hot practice field and perform at the very best of my ability without complaining or griping about it.'"

Each time Rick read *He Leadeth Me* it reminded him that no matter how hot, tired, and painful the two-a-day practices might be, they could not begin to approach the ordeal that Fr. Ciszek endured for twenty–three years! As you are reading the book, with each paragraph, you will think, "How did he survive this, and then this, and this?" The only answer can be found in Fr. Ciszek's own words,

> For what can ultimately trouble the soul that accepts every moment of every day as a gift from the hands of God and strives always to do his will? If God is for us, who can stand against us? Nothing, not even death, can separate us from God. Nothing can touch us that does not come from his hand, nothing can trouble us because all things come from his hand. Is this too simple, or are we just afraid really to believe it, to accept it fully and in every detail of our lives, to yield ourselves up to it in total commitment? This is the ultimate question of faith,

and each must answer it for himself in the quiet of his heart and the depths of his soul. But to answer it in the affirmative is to know a peace, to discover a meaning to life, that surpasses all understanding. (Walter Ciszek, SJ, *He Leadeth Me*, Ignatius)

After all of those NFL preseason camps spent with Fr. Ciszek, Rick said, "The reality that this moment is exactly where God wants me to be and is exactly the time and place for me to encounter Him, was an eye opening revelation. God is not far off. He's not over there. He's right in my circumstances no matter what they are, where I am, and He is available to me for this intimate relationship." Fr. Ciszek had taught him that he did not need to look for, or discern, God's will. He had come to know that this moment is God's will. This moment is perfect.

If you remember back to chapters six and seven, peak performances occur when athletes focus 100 percent of their skills, talents, and abilities on the task at hand, in the present moment. That's as good as it gets in athletics. Now consider that, to God, all of time is present. He has no past and he has no future. When we ruminate about the past or become anxious about the future we have left him. Therefore, the degree to which we remain in the present moment, is the degree to which we remain in perfect union with him. It is a great comfort and wonder to know that when we perform in the present moment in sport or life, we are closest to him.

And it is in that present moment that you are best able to listen. Amidst all the clutter and noise, God is talking to you. He is asking you to do something with the gifts that he has given you. There is probably no better story than the parable of the talents to understand what that is.

It will be as when a man who was going on a journey
called in his servants and entrusted his possessions to

them. To one he gave five talents;* to another, two; to a third, one—to each according to his ability. Then he went away. Immediately the one who received five talents went and traded with them, and made another five. Likewise, the one who received two made another two. But the man who received one went off and dug a hole in the ground and buried his master's money. After a long time the master of those servants came back and settled accounts with them. The one who had received five talents came forward bringing the additional five. He said, "Master, you gave me five talents. See, I have made five more." His master said to him, "Well done, my good and faithful servant. Since you were faithful in small matters, I will give you great responsibilities. Come, share your master's joy." [Then] the one who had received two talents also came forward and said, "Master, you gave me two talents. See, I have made two more." His master said to him, "Well done, my good and faithful servant. Since you were faithful in small matters, I will give you great responsibilities. Come, share your master's joy." Then the one who had received the one talent came forward and said, "Master, I knew you were a demanding person, harvesting where you did not plant and gathering where you did not scatter; so out of fear I went off and buried your talent in the ground. Here it is back." His master said to him in reply, "You wicked, lazy servant! So you knew that I harvest where I did not plant and gather where I did not scatter? Should you not then have put my

---

* Talents were typically silver or gold bars that weighed between fifty and one hundred pounds and would have represented an extraordinary sum. One talent of gold weighing seventy-five pounds would be worth over 1.8 million dollars in today's market. Five talents would be valued at well over 9 million dollars.

money in the bank so that I could have got it back with interest on my return? Now then! Take the talent from him and give it to the one with ten. For to everyone who has, more will be given and he will grow rich; but from the one who has not, even what he has will be taken away. And throw this useless servant into the darkness outside, where there will be wailing and grinding of teeth."

It is worth noting that each servant was given a different measure of silver, each according to his ability, but each one was asked to do the same thing with it, to double it. How often does the world try to pretend that everything is equal and that everyone is the same? Being different is not a bad thing. In the parable of the talents God shows you that if you double whatever He has given you, big or small, the reward is the same. By your fidelity and perseverance in doing this, you will be brought into perfect union with Him and hear the most comforting of words, "Good and faithful servant, enter into your Master's joy."

One of the challenges in life is to know whether or not you are in the process of doubling your talents. Not the gold or silver kind referred to in the parable, but the skills, talents, and abilities God has entrusted you with while he is away. Too often we can mistake being better than others for having doubled our talents. You might be tempted to look around and compare yourself to others and ask, "Am I winning or losing? Am I better than they are?"

You may be delighted when you learn that you have accomplished much more than those around you; but before you start strutting around thinking, "I am just like that guy with the five talents," you might want to very carefully consider what you were given. Otherwise, you might find yourself on judgment day standing before the gates of Heaven with a gallon jug of water. Having just arrived, you see five people ahead of you, each holding a thimble full of water. As they approach the pearly gates, their thimbles are checked. One by one they enter into Heaven. Finally, it's your turn. With some pride and a smile slowly spreading across your face, you lift the heavy gallon jug and, without pausing, attempt to continue on. Suddenly the gates shut and a voice calls you back. "Where are you going?" "Into Heaven of course," you say. "I'm sorry but you did nothing with what I gave you," admonishes the voice. "But you let those people in with thimbles; I have a gallon," you demur. "Yes," says the voice, "But that is all they were given. Turn around." When you turn, there behind you is the Atlantic Ocean. The voice says, "That is what I gave you but all you have brought with you is this gallon jug."

To those who have been given much, much will be demanded. It does not matter if you are the world record holder if it is less than you were meant to be. Roberto Clemente, a member of the Baseball Hall of Fame who died at the age of thirty-eight while personally delivering desperately needed supplies to the victims of a massive earthquake in Nicaragua said, "Any time you have an opportunity to make a difference in this world and you don't, then you are wasting your time here on Earth."

Doubling your talents is not about earning your way into Heaven. It's about the higher argument made in the Act of Contrition. It's about responding to God's love and grace in your life. Even when you do, doubling all that you have been given, you are still like a little child in the eyes of God. This is probably a good thing since God loves little children; maybe that's why we love children so much, too. Have you ever been given a drawing by a young child? She usually walks up to you with a smile that can't be contained. She is bursting with joy and the anticipation of giving you her work of love, her masterpiece. From behind her back, with sudden quickness, a drawing is thrust at you. "I made this for you," she beams. Her joy has you smiling before you have even seen it. Conscious that she is carefully studying your reaction, you immediately say, "Oh, my! This is extraordinary! Did you really do this yourself?" She looks down in humility and says, "Yes, and I made it just for you."

The reality is that as you look at the drawing, you have no idea what it is. There appear to be some creatures that could be human but it's hard to know for sure. If someone had found it on the street they would have thrown it away. So you say, "Well, this is just incredible, tell me all about it." She goes on to tell you, "This is you and me walking in the garden, and Mom and Dad are on the roof of the house waving to us, and they have balloons and a cake for your birthday, and there are seagulls flying around like when we were at the beach . . ." The entire time you listen with rapt attention and when she looks up from the picture you gaze into her eyes in awe of the pure and innocent love before you. There is only one thing to do, you say, "We must hang this up on the refrigerator." Of course this is the equivalent of hanging it in the Louvre. She trails excitedly behind you towards the fridge where your happiness and her love will be on display for the world to see.

In the eyes of God you are a lot like the little girl. Your life is your drawing and at the end of your time you will bring it to him and with a beaming smile say, "I made this for you!" God will look at it like you looked at hers, despite being a composite of scribbled lines, he will say, "Oh, my! This is extraordinary! Did you really do this yourself?" You will look down in humility and say, "Yes, though I now know you helped me along the way. I made it just for you." God will say, "There is only one thing to do. We must hang it on the refrigerator." And there, infinite happiness and love will hang for eternity.

Here are three clues to ensure that your picture ends up on the refrigerator. The first is that God exists. This may not be so hard for you to believe since a recent Gallup poll showed that over 92 percent of Americans believe in God. If God exists, it means that there is automatically some kind of a connection or relationship between you and God. It doesn't mean that you are necessarily doing anything about it, but that wouldn't change the fact that there is a connection, however remote. Just because you can't see the moon at this moment doesn't mean it doesn't exist. If God exists, you not believing in Him or doing anything about it doesn't change the fact that he exists. Assuming you are in the 92 percent, or at least open to the idea that there really is a God, what's next?

The second clue is that you've only been given one thing. Everything else can be taken away from you in a fraction of a second: your life, your health, your family, your home, your car, your legs, and on and on. Boom! Gone in an instant. All you are left with is how you are going to deal with it. The only thing you really have been given is your free will. You might wonder, "Why free will? Why have I been given this ability to decide how I will act and react to things?" Think of it this way. What if you were told that, in a few moments, you were going to meet some-one who is being paid five thousand dollars a day to say that they love you. They walk in, look you in the eye, and with dramatic flair say, "I love you." Does it mean anything to you? Probably not, because you know they are being paid to say it.

Now imagine that God walks into the room, Are you going to leave the room? Is anyone going to leave the room? No! God looks at you and asks, "Do you love me?" How are you going to answer? You're going to say, "Yes!" You might think, "What about the atheists?" Well, God is in the room. There are no more atheists. So even the atheist, if asked by God, "Do you love me?" is going to say, perhaps with some embarrassment, "Yes!", because he knows the consequence of saying no.

However, at this point it doesn't mean as much as having said it before seeing the Truth. Like the guy with the five thou-sand dollars, you're almost feeling compelled to say, "Yes." It's like getting married with a gun held to your head while saying your vows; it doesn't count. It isn't valid because you did not freely choose to marry. The reason you were given free will is so that you could choose to love. Without it, you are not capable of truly loving anyone including God.

The third clue, at the risk of sounding morbid, is that we are all going to die. There has never been a person who hasn't died. The question is, "How long are you going to live?" Seventy years? Eighty? Ninety? Maybe, one hundred? Be optimistic and say that you will live to be one hundred years old. Now—sorry to do this to you—imagine the worst possible pain. Do you have something? Okay, now snap your finger once in less than a second. Go ahead and actually try it! Now snap it in less than half a second. Good! Now, one hundredth of a second. A thousandth of a second. A millionth of a second. Still going? Let's make it ridiculous, a billionth of a second. Can you even move that fast?

Clearly it's not possible but it's to your credit if you're still trying! Now recall that worst possible pain you imagined earlier. If it would come and go in one billionth of a second, with no aftereffect at all, could you take it? Most people say, "Yes, it's so fast that I wouldn't be able to feel it or even know I had it." Go back to the age question. You said you might live until you were one hundred years old. How long is one hundred years in relation to all of eternity, all of time? In essence it's shorter than a billionth of a second and you just said you could take the worst pain in the world for a billionth of a second. That's your life.

God is asking you just one question: "Do you love me?" He puts you here on this earth for the shortest possible time, less than a billionth of a second, and asks if you will choose to love him. It's almost embarrassing—imagine going home to someone you love and asking, "Would you love me for a billionth of a second?" They'd think you're out of your mind. And yet God, in His infinite mercy, puts you here for less-than-a-billionth-of-a-second and says, "I'm giving you free will and I am asking you one question, 'Do you love me?'" Of course, you can give the lip service and say, "Oh yeah, I love you. Of course I love you." But the way you really know people in the end is not by what they say but by what they do. You hope what they say matches what they do but in the end it is their actions that speak louder than their words.

The same holds true for you. God plops you down somewhere on earth with your particular family and socio-economic background, and He says, "I am going to give you opportunities to sacrifice." How you respond to them determines your answer to His question, "Do you love me?" When you choose to take on the sacrifice you have said, "Yes." The times you look away are the times that you have said, "No." The way you live out your life is the answer to the single most important question you will ever be asked, "Do you love me?"

TAKE AWAY

Your life is faster than a billionth of a second. Knowing what is most important in life, your strongest purpose, will enable you to accept and make the sacrifices necessary to double your talents. By living, working, and playing in the present moment you will experience peak performances and remain in perfect union with God. Your love in thought, word, and deed for God and neighbor is the answer to the most important question that you will ever be asked: "Do you love me?" Are you ready to live it?

ABOUT THE AUTHOR

Dr. Bill Thierfelder is President of Belmont Abbey College, a Catholic Liberal Arts College located 10 miles west of Charlotte, NC. Founded by Benedictine monks over 137 years ago, the College embodies the Benedictine tradition of prayer and learning by educating its students to lead lives of integrity, succeed professionally, become responsible citizens, and be a blessing to themselves and others.

Dr. Thierfelder received his master's and doctoral degrees in Sports Psychology and Human Movement from Boston University. He is a licensed psychologist and a Diplomate of the American Board of Psychological Specialties. He is also a member of the American College of Sports Medicine. He is a former member of the United States Olympic Committee's Sport Psychology Registry, an NCAA Division I Coach, Olympian (did not compete due to injury), National Champion (IRE) and a two-time All-American from the University of Maryland. He is a member of the Sports Faith International Hall of Fame, which includes world-class athletes, coaches, and team owners such as George "Papa Bear" Halas, Wellington Mara, Brian Piccolo, and others.

Prior to his appointment as President of Belmont Abbey College, Dr. Thierfelder was president of the legendary fitness company York Barbell. Other career posts include Executive Director of the Player Management Group, National Director of Sports Science for Nova-Care, and principal and cofounder of Joyner Sports Medicine Institute; where he helped over a hundred Olympic and professional athletes achieve dramatic improvements in performance.

Dr. Thierfelder has delivered hundreds of presentations on topics related to faith, sport, education, medicine and business, as well as testifying before the United States Congress on matters related to religious liberty. He is a Knight of Malta and lives just outside of Charlotte, NC with his wife, Mary and their ten children.

SAINT BENEDICT✠PRESS

Saint Benedict Press publishes books, Bibles, and multimedia that explore and defend the Catholic intellectual tradition. Our mission is to present the truths of the Catholic faith in an attractive and accessible manner.

Founded in 2006, our name pays homage to the guiding influence of the Rule of Saint Benedict and the Benedictine monks of Belmont Abbey, just a short distance from our headquarters in Charlotte, NC.

Saint Benedict Press publishes under several imprints. Our TAN Books imprint (TANBooks.com), publishes over 500 titles in theology, spirituality, devotions, Church doctrine, history, and the Lives of the Saints. Our Catholic Courses imprint (CatholicCourses.com) publishes audio and video lectures from the world's best professors in Theology, Philosophy, Scripture, Literature and more.

For a free catalog, visit us online at
TANBooks.com

Or call us toll-free at
(800) 437-5876

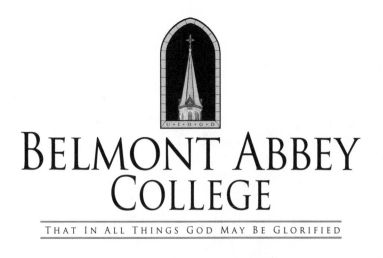

BELMONT ABBEY
COLLEGE
THAT IN ALL THINGS GOD MAY BE GLORIFIED

Belmont Abbey College finds its center in Jesus Christ and believes in the development of the whole person—in mind, body and spirit. Founded in 1876 by Benedictine monks, the College, located just 10 miles west of Charlotte, N.C., is currently home to more than 1600 students.

The Newman Guide calls Belmont Abbey College one of the top Catholic colleges in America for faithfulness and affordability, and *First Things* Magazine recently named the Abbey America's #1 "School On The Rise, Filled With Excitement." Consistently ranked as one of the best liberal arts institutions in the South, the College enjoys an outstanding academic reputation.

Imagine a place where every person is committed to perfecting the intellectual, moral and theological virtues in their life as well as helping others to do the same. Come experience first-hand Belmont Abbey's 137 year tradition of hospitality, personal attention and teaching excellence.

**To learn more about us, visit us online at
BelmontAbbeyCollege.edu**

**Or call us at
1-888-222-0110.**

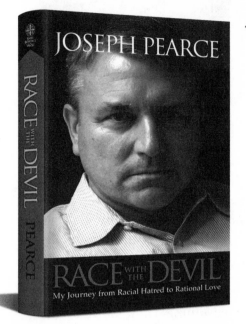

CATHOLIC COURSES

Learn More

True Friendship

Where Virtue Becomes Happiness

Professor John Cuddeback, Ph.D.

True Friendship:
Where Virtue Becomes Happiness

John Cuddeback, Ph.D.

Courage, fortitude, wisdom, charity . . . what do these virtues have to do with friendship?

Being virtuous, says Aristotle, is how man becomes happy. If we want real friendship, we must first become the kind of person one would want to be friends with.

Course No. C10
ISBN: 978-1-61890-042-

Professor Cuddeback deftly weaves together the age-old wisdom of the Greeks and the fundamental teachings of Sacred Scripture to reveal the most rewarding of human achievements—being a friend. He takes the thoughts of the great philosopher Aristotle, the Angelic Doctor St. Thomas Aquinas, and the sublime teachings of Jesus Christ to illustrate the nature and requirements of true friendship.

Join Professor Cuddeback to discover what friendship is, why we seek it, why good friends are so often hard to find, and how to make the friends (and be the friend) you've always desired.

Professor John Cuddeback, Ph.D.

EIGHT LECTURES
(30 minutes per lecture)

DVD Set	$89.95	$59.95
Video Download	$69.95	$49.95
Audio CD	$59.95	$39.95
Audio Download	$39.95	$29.95

CATHOLIC COURSES is an innovative approach to capturing and delivering the riches of our Catholic intellectual heritage. We partner with the best professors and scholars of the Church today, to deliver relevant, faithful courses in HD quality audio and video series.

CatholicCourses.com • (800) 437-5876